MODERN
ISLAMIC WARFARE

MODERN
ISLAMIC
WARFARE

An Ancient Doctrine
Marches On

By Harold Rhode

Center for Security Policy Press

For more information about this book, visit
SecureFreedom.org

Modern Islamic Warfare is published in the United States
by the Center for Security Policy Press,
a division of the Center for Security Policy.

ISBN-13: 978-1548095697
ISBN-10: 1548095699

The Center for Security Policy
Washington, D.C.
Phone: 202-835-9077
Email: info@SecureFreedom.org
For more information, visit SecureFreedom.org

Book design by Bravura Books
Cover design by J.P. Zarruk

On the cover

SIEGE OF VIENNA, 1683. Forces commanded by Charles V, Duke of Lorraine,
and John III Sobieski, King of Poland, drive back the Turkish Muslim armies
besieging Vienna in 1683. Detail of painting by Frans Geffels.

The implements of war and the context of battle change over time, but the core
theological principles of Islamic warfare remain the same over the centuries.

Contents

To Professor Bernard Lewis,
as wise as he is kind,
who taught me how to think about
the Muslim world;

To Richard Perle,
who believed in me and gave me a chance
to implement what I had learned
about Turkey and the Middle East;

To Ahmad, Alex, David, Ephi, Jonny, and Yossi,
who have been among my greatest
advocates and sharpest critics;

And to my wife Judith,
who for decades has supported my endeavors
to try to find a way to make peace
with the Muslim world.

FOREWORD

For all the effort that the United States and our allies around the world have put into taking on the Islamic jihad enemy since the attacks of September 11, 2001, there has been a startling absence in the academic literature of analysis about not just who this enemy is and why he fights us, but also about *how* he fights. With several notable—and laudable—exceptions, few have delved deeply into the merciless, systematic, and ongoing methods of classic Islamic warfare that date back to medieval times in order to understand the nature, concepts and philosophy that have combined over the centuries with such deadly effectiveness to defeat brilliant civilizations like the Byzantines, Hindus, and Persians.

Knowing that Western civilization has been for many centuries squarely in the sights of the Global Islamic Movement—with countless engagements large and small on battlefields across the globe attesting to the implacable will of the Islamic enemy to defeat and subjugate us—it would seem to behoove us to examine the cultural, military, political, religious and social currents within Islam that inspire its relentless drive for supremacy. Even more specifically, if we are to avoid the fate of countless others who have succumbed to this onslaught, we need also to study and confront the Islamic style of warfare.

That is particularly true insofar as the 21st Century is shaping up to be a time of accelerating attacks by the forces of Islam. Much of that takes the form of unconventional warfare, as has been true in the past, as well. An Islamic state that takes, holds and claims to govern territory it calls a Caliphate remains the ultimate ideal for Muslim warriors. ISIS' "Caliph" Abu Bakr al Baghdadi and followers have simply brought to bear for this purpose the modern-day equivalents of camels, horses, swords, spears, catapults and mangonels. Their instruments of jihad include blitzkrieg-style charges across vast desert expanses in captured U.S. Humvees, armored cars and machine-gun-mounted pickup trucks; artillery, the use of automatic rifles, rockets, missiles and mortars in fire-and-maneuver warfare; and deadly attacks with Improvised Explosive Devices (IEDs) and car bombs.

Violent Islamic warfare is increasingly evident in the *Dar al-Harb*—the non-Islamic West—where it is augmenting and exacerbating the danger posed by the stealthy, *pre*-violent form long practiced there by the Muslim Brotherhood, which calls it "civilization jihad." More and

1

more, Europe and the United States are being subjected to such asymmetric techniques as: airliners brought down with explosives secreted in a laptop; individual suicide bombings; or random acts of violence inflicted with knives, guns and vehicles used to mow down pedestrians.

The Internet, too, has revolutionized modern Islamic warfare by allowing jihadist commanders, imams, jurists and strategists to disseminate diagrams, encouragement, guidance and instructions, both inspirational and operational, throughout the world, often reaching huge global audiences. Ever-more clandestine means of evading discovery through the use, for example of, crypto-currencies, the Dark Web and sophisticated cyber encryption programs all too often keep jihadis many steps ahead of the security experts trying to stop them.

Unfortunately, we must expect to be facing such attacks from the Global Jihad Movement for a long time to come. To help us understand what we are up against, the Center for Security Policy is pleased to present this new monograph in our Terror Jihad Reader Series, "Modern Islamic Warfare," written by one of the top Middle Eastern scholars of our time. Dr. Harold Rhode is a Distinguished Senior Fellow at the Gatestone Institute and a Middle East specialist who worked as a highly regarded Pentagon analyst for almost 30 years, observing and participating directly in crafting and implementing U.S. Middle East policy throughout those three decades. He's also an extraordinary linguist who speaks Arabic, Farsi, Hebrew and Turkish. Dr. Rhode has been inspired in his own scholarship by one of the giants of Middle Eastern studies, Dr. Bernard Lewis, his close friend and mentor of many years.

We hope that "Modern Islamic Warfare" will contribute materially to our understanding of the strategy and tactics of the forces of Sharia-supremacism and the jihad it commands. Equipped with Harold Rhode's important insights, we will be better able to help formulate and implement an effective national security strategy for defeating that enemy and his totalitarian ambitions.

Frank Gaffney
President and CEO
Center for Security Policy
30 May 2017

OVERVIEW

lassic Islamic warfare integrates cultural attributes of early Arab and Bedouin tribes with the moral dimension of Islam. Consisting of a long series of conquests and re-captures—which combine military force, political pressure, and cultural intimidation—the overall aim is to end the sovereignty and supremacy of the unbelievers, who are seen as innately evil.

Today, in many Muslim countries, there are powerful movements—state-sponsored and otherwise—that are motivated by a similar ideology, resurgent Islam, which blames secularism and modernism for robbing them of their dignity, beliefs, and success. And they have adapted their ancestors' medieval designs to reflect modern times.

The original Islamic warriors optimized tactical advantages, including deception, intimidation, and assassination, to compensate for their relative ineffectiveness in conventional combat against larger forces in Arabia and elsewhere. Likewise, today's Islamic soldiers pursue unconventional warfare, employing hijackings, suicide bombings, and other terrorist tactics to create asymmetries and subdue superior foes in the West.

It is this classical version of Islamic warfare—merciless, systematic, and ongoing—which the United States and its democratic allies will likely continuously encounter in the coming decades. It is urgently necessary for policymakers to comprehend this endeavor. For that reason, this report provides an overview of classic Islamic warfare—examining key concepts and specific philosophies within Islam, which have provided religious, social, and political support for violence and terrorism against the West.

From a Muslim point of view, Islam is engaged in an unending battle which will continue until either Muslims rule the entire world or the rest of the world utterly defeats Islam. It is important to note that as it is extremely difficult to find universal agreement on the differences between "normative" Islam and what today many refer to as "radical" or "fundamentalist" Islam. In this book, we will refer to it simply as "Islam." Presented here is an array of observations, implications, and recommendations—policy options which will hopefully improve the development of America's strategy and tactics, aid in the pursuit of diplomatic and coalition building initiatives, and correct the trajectory of the War on Terror.

INTRODUCTION

Many officials in the West, including former President Barack Obama, have declared Islam is "a religion of peace." However, Islamic doctrine provides emphasis, symbolism, and rule of law to the Islamic State's violent proceedings. Does this mean that modern jihadists do not follow the Islam as it is written or as it was intended by Mohammad to be practiced? Can Islamic doctrine be re-interpreted, or is it immutable?

Furthermore, polling in numerous Muslim-majority countries—the Arab Middle East included—shows that, even among Muslims who reject violence, significant percentages adhere to beliefs that run contrary to our liberal, democratic principles. So, even if it's permissible to challenge the fundamental claims established by Islamic doctrine, who is capable of doing so without alienating vast numbers of believers to whom they are appealing?

The assumption that the vast majority of Muslims can be won over to Western democracy is premised on the conceit that Western values are universal and, hence, locatable in the core of Islam. However, is Islam reconcilable with the Western tradition of individual freedom and religious liberty? And if so, can anyone accurately identify the existence of a coherent "moderate Islam?" What is the litmus test?

Many scholars have written books and articles on classic Islamic warfare.[1] They contain extremely detailed information showing how the classic Islamic scholars understood and formulated the rules of war. But how relevant are they today? And do today's jihadists abide by the rules laid out by those jurists? Today's jihadists claim to be fighting "in the way of their prophet Muhammad." But are they?

Do today's jihadis follow the Islamic law? Are they within Islamic tradition? Who defines what is or is not Islamic? Why do Muslims living in the West almost never condemn the barbarism committed by Muslims in the name of Islam? Why is that Western leaders—recently and most notably President Obama—constantly claim that Islam is a religion of peace, while so many Muslims disagree? Who can make this decision? Is Islam a religion of peace?

---

[1] Among the best is Majid Khadduri's annotated translation of the 8th century classic "The Islamic Law of Nations: Shaybani's Siyar." https://www.amazon.com/Islamic-Law-Nations-Shaybanis-Siyar/dp/0801869757

Islam is not just a religion. It is a civilization which certainly includes religion but also includes important political and military dimensions. In order to understand the true nature of Islam, therefore, it would be more useful to label it an ideology.

Our problems with Islam are not religious. From our point of view, everyone has the right to practice whatever religion he wants. We in the West strongly hesitate to get involved in other peoples' religions and relationships with the supernatural.

But we do have serious problems with the political and military nature of Islam. These are uncompromising. From an Islamic point of view, there can never be permanent peace between the non-Muslim world and Islam. Islam recognizes only two political entities: 1. Dar al-Islam (The Abode of Islam)—*i.e.*, the world where Muslims rule; 2. Dar al-Harb (The Abode of War), which is the permanent target of the Muslims. According to classic Islamic texts, there is a permanent battle between these two worlds which will end only when the Muslims conquer the entire world. There cannot be peace between these two worlds—only temporary truces. Muslims can do whatever they must in order to bring the entire world under Islamic rule.

Even so, that does not mean that all Muslims agree on who should rule this entire world when it eventually becomes Muslim. Muslims have historically had no problems killing other Muslims, as will be explained below.

It is disconcerting that we non-Muslims on the outside are actually taking the bait—addressing each new tactic/issue the Muslims bring up, instead of understanding the problem for what it is—Islam's unwillingness to accept that there is another narrative—not theirs—which must be taken into consideration. Instead of attacking head on the problem we face—the unwillingness for the Muslim to live in peace with the non-Muslim world—we mistakenly insist on addressing each and every one of the problems the Muslim powers bring up.

Our mistake is to respond to each accusation, which misses the point of what is going on (*i.e.*, the larger context).

Jihad

Jihad has become the hot topic around so much of the discussion about how to understand what the fanatic Muslims are doing today. Historically, jihad conjured up one and almost only one thing to the Muslim mind: Expanding Islam, *i.e.*, conquering new territories bringing them under Islamic rule. We can see how Islam started as a small tribal confederation around Mecca and Medina in today's Saudi Arabia and, within fewer than 100 years, controlled an area from the Chinese wall westward all the way to today's Spain and Portugal. That was an amazing accomplishment, and can be attributed to many factors. But from a Muslim point of view, that meant that Allah was clearly on the side of the Muslims, because there could have been no other explanation why Islam has such a remarkable success.

As these territories were brought under Islamic rule, with time, most of the peoples living in these territories converted to Islam. As Islam expanded, those new territories on the periphery became the battlegrounds for the next waves of Islamic expansion.

Jihad was—and still is—an essential part of Islam. Some scholars have actually argued that jihad is the sixth basic pillar of Islam. (The five being Shahada (the declaration of faith), Hajj to Mecca, fasting during the month of Ramadan, Zakat (Giving Alms), and Salat (Prayer).

Every important classical Islamic scholar wrote a chapter on the importance of jihad. Whether it is or is not part of the basic tenets of that religion, all agree that bringing Islam to the entire world is one of the most important principles in Islam.

Whatever the case, it cannot be ignored. That is why so many of the Muslim apologists and Muslims who want to neutralize Western criticism of Islam, argue that there is the internal jihad—*i.e.*, one's personal duty to make himself a better person. While some Muslim scholars have historically mentioned this, most do not. Indeed, most classical scholars would have found the use of the word jihad for personal improvement as, at best, a minor meaning of the word, if they used the word "jihad" at all in this context.

Yet in the Muslim context, where almost anything is acceptable in order to propagate Islam, playing with the meanings of words is at best a minor irritant. What matters is to pacify the non-Muslim enemies ruling the Dar al-Harb (the World of War) in any way possible, so that the

Muslims—á la Hudaybiyyah,[2] can eventually resume the fight to bring the whole world under Islamic rule.

At our peril, we often neglect the symbolism that other countries and cultures use. For example, Saudi Arabia's flag makes clear exactly what the Saudis, as Guardians of the two most holy cities—Mecca and Medina—have in store for the world. The flag has a green background, which is supposed to be their prophet Muhammad's most favorite color. In fact, the Qur'an describes paradise as a place where cushions and garments are lush green colors. (Could this be because Islam came into existence born in the harsh Arabian dessert which overwhelmingly lacked the lush green vegetation so necessary for survival?)

But more importantly, the Saudi flag has the Muslim "pledge of alliance" called the Shahada—*i.e.*, the basic creed of Islam written in beautiful white calligraphy in the middle "There is no god but Allah, and Muhammad is his messenger."

But the essential point is the white sword below the calligraphy. Why the sword? Because a principal goal of Islam is to conquer the world by the sword. This is why the territories conquered in the first hundred years of Islam became bases to expand, and conquer the new territories for Islam just across the border.

The previously mentioned Dar al-Harb—*i.e.*, is, according to the sharia (Islamic Law)[3], to be the focus of jihad, and it is never-ending until the entire world becomes Muslim. So in essence, the World of War, in Islamic terms, can better be described as the world not yet Muslim, but which will eventually be brought under Muslim rule. So much for letting others chose their own way.

Throughout history, various Islamic figures have interpreted jihad as they saw fit. This malleability has enabled the Muslims to use this concept creatively to cover any necessity. For example, when the leaders of one Muslim country wanted to attack their Muslim neighbors,

---

[2] Muhammad fought the Quraysh tribe from Mecca at a place called Hudaybiyyah in 628 CE. He and his enemies declared a ten-year ceasefire. Muhammad and his forces used the time to rearm. Two years after the signing of the truce, Muhammad, believing he was now strong enough to defeat his enemies, violated the truce and defeated the Quraysh. Since then, Muslims have imitated Muhammad's strategy here, i.e., when the Muslims were weak, they declared a ceasefire, which we in the West have all too often labeled a peace treaty. But the Muslims don't see it as such. It's just an interregnum so they can militarily regroup and defeat their enemies. As we will see later, there is no concept of permanent peace in Islam. For more on the Hudaybiyyah agreement and its importance in Islam, see https://en.wikipedia.org/wiki/Treaty_of_Hudaybiyyah

[3] i.e., Islamic law, based on the Quran and the Hadiths. But the Sunnis and Shi'ites do not accept the same hadiths and even understand the Quran differently. For more on Sharia, see, the Encyclopedia of Islam entry Shari'a, and https://en.wikipedia.org/wiki/Sharia.

they would go to their religious authorities and have them issue a *fatwa* (*i.e.*, a religious decree), labeling the leader or leaders of a neighboring Muslim state as apostates or non-Muslims. As the punishment for apostasy in Islam is death, this declaration enabled one Muslim country to declare war on the other. Moreover, this declaration allowed rulers to side-step the Islamic dictum that all Muslims are brothers.

These various interpretations of the word *"jihad"* has also been useful today in pacifying or trying to make Western leaders not resist Islamic attacks and undermining their resistance. These Muslims have been so successful that even under the George W. Bush administration—thought to be much more willing to confront Islam—senior officials went out of their way to try to find ways not to criticize *"jihad"* because they had been informed by many of the Muslims they chose to label "moderate" that *jihad* had very positive associations in Islam, and therefore, we had to do our best to get around this word, for fear of "offending the Muslims."

It is in this context that we must understand Yassir Arafat and his PLO, Hamas, Hizballah, and the government of the Islamic Republic of Iran. All of them made it clear, their mission is jihad, which meant both the reclamation of formerly Islamic territory for Islam, and the expansion of Islam in any way necessary so that the entire world would become Muslim.[4,5,6,7] We in the non-Muslim world ignore what they tell us in their documents and in their speeches at our peril.

In that same vein, in addition, Bush administration officials spent hundreds of hours debating how to label the war against the forces of Islamic jihad and sharia by any other words other than using the word "Islam." That required putting their staffs through all sorts of mental gyrations and machinations, where eventually some bureaucrats eventually invented the term GWOT (Global War on Terrorism).

---

[4] See the Iranian Constitution: the Army of the Islamic Republic of Iran and the Islamic Revolutionary Guards Corps are to be organized in conformity with this goal, and they will be responsible not only for guarding and preserving the frontiers of the country, but also for fulfilling the ideological mission of jihad in God's way; that is, extending the sovereignty of God's law throughout the world (this is in accordance with the Koranic verse *"Prepare against them whatever force you are able to muster, and strings of horses, striking fear into the enemy of God and your enemy, and others besides them"* [8:60]).

[5] See Arafat's speech on Jihad two weeks after he signed the Oslo Accords on the White lawn.

[6] See Hamas's Covenant, https://www.jewishvirtuallibrary.org/hamas-covenant-full-text

[7] Lewis, Bernard, "Notes of a Century", May 2013, https://www.amazon.com/Notes-Century-Reflections-Middle-Historian/dp/1455890790

One must admire the masterful creativity their Muslim Brotherhood advisors used to get them to avoid labeling the enemy for what it was—normative Islam. But when at war, it is essential that soldiers know who their enemy is and what they are fighting against. Otherwise, one is fighting against windmills and has no chance of defeating their enemies. As the great Middle Eastern historian Bernard Lewis reminds us: "The British were not engaged in a war against U-boats; they were fighting a war against the Nazis." As such, it is critical that we, too, identify our enemy—which is all who fight or support jihad to establish a global Islamic Caliphate under rule of Islamic Law (sharia). Not all Muslims are obedient to the commandments of their own faith, but certainly sharia comes out of Islam and expresses Islam's definition of itself, including the Islamic doctrine of jihad. We are not fighting against an ideology. We are fighting against people who subscribe to that ideology.

In the 7th century Arabian Peninsula, men were responsible for providing for their families and their clans. As such, they developed sophisticated methods of capturing animals, rules for water and oases, and interactions with other tribes.

Life revolved around families, clans, and tribes, each of which had their particular responsibilities towards each other, and towards their enemies. Personal friendships outside the social unit structure were secondary to group loyalty. People as such were most concerned about their group's standing—in Arabic, *sharaf*—than anything else. The group's honor mattered more than land.[8]

Losing men meant losing the ability to provide for the family and the clan, so it was important to find methods to limit the number of deaths in war. As such, in pre-Islamic Arabia, warfare occurred between small groups. In order to preserve life and prevent death in battles between clans, tribes etc., the Arabs developed fine poetic skills. Instead of physically fighting, the opposing sides often sent their best poets to resent them, each trying to "out-humiliate" the other. The side which most eloquently did so was declared the winner. Thus their meager human resources were spared for the next battle. While this might seem

---

[8] There is a classical Arabic rhyming proverb which sums this up beautifully: *"al-ard qabl al-'ard"* – (meaning one's personal honor is more important than one's land.

unrelated to warfare, it in fact served as a way to preserve life in ancient Arabia.

Humiliation and shame were understood to be fates worse than death — as they still are today, which is why Muslims so often prefer death to public humiliation and cannot compromise. Personal, clan, tribal and honor are an all-or-nothing process. One cannot be partially humiliated. Even if one suffers a minor insult, he must look for the opportunity to avenge that insult, which must be eventually righted, even if it takes generations to do so.

Compromise is understood as humiliation, which is why political agreements between Muslims and other Muslims or non-Muslims are so difficult to reach. That is also why one almost never encounters Middle Eastern leaders who are prepared to compromise. From their perspective, compromise means you have given in, *i.e.,* someone else has dominated you, a fate you must avoid at all costs. Honor goes only to the winner.

When violence occurred between warring tribes, from what we know, it was almost always small raiding parties that raided their enemies, the goal of which was to strike fear and terror into their enemies' hearts, and then withdraw. They would do this over and over again until their enemies fled, and the victors would take the spoils that their enemies left behind.

This Pre-Islamic Arabian war culture is the ancient precursor of modern terrorism. This form of warfare—*i.e.*, raiding the enemy and retreating—has not been the major form of warfare in the West for many centuries. Western warfare entailed large armies, capturing territory, and especially the country's/empire's capital, which we understand as victory. Though this happened from time to time, it is not how Muslims practiced warfare. **Neither capturing territory nor seizing the enemy's capital meant capitulation and loss.** The vanquished simply retreated to another place and set up its new headquarters or capital. This, for example, is exactly what happened in the battle between the Ottomans and the Safavids in Iran. The Safavid capital was Tabriz, the large city in today's Iranian Azerbaijan. But when the Ottomans captured it in the 1510s, the Safavids simply retreated and moved their capital to Isfahan in Central Iran, and did not capitulate to the Ottomans.

That is why the Western concept of surrender and compromise are alien in the Muslim world. That is why Saddam never admitted defeat, and why he could not ever give in to American threats that he would lose his empire/fiefdom (Iraq) if he did not back down. Middle Easterners cannot and do not back down. They would rather die than admit defeat.

How Do Today's Jihadis Understand Themselves?

Today's jihadis pattern their behavior on how they understand their prophet's actions and those of his companions. They look to the biography of their prophet—called the *Sira*—whose author ibn Ishaq belonged to their prophet's grandchildren's generation. Sunnis accept the *Sira* as authentic. The author did not know Muhammad, but heard stories about him and his grandfather's generation while growing up. Today's jihadis are emulating the description of Muhammad and his fighters that which they learn about from the *Sira*. The methods the jihads use both in warfare and in decapitating their opponents closely resemble those described in the *Sira*.

The fighting described in this biography closely resembles the methods of warfare the Arab tribes practiced in pre-Islamic Arabia. Therefore, in order to understand how the jihadis think about warfare, we must understand the context in which Islam developed. Islam came into existence in the Arabia which life was extremely difficult.

From what we are witnessing today, today's Islamic warriors do not read, nor do they seem to care much about what their legal ancestors wrote. They rely on the interpretations of whichever contemporary legal authority suits their needs. Moreover, there is no central authority which can issue *fatwas* that the Muslims believe they must abide by. *So, there is no central authority which can speak for Islam.*

Indeed, Sunnis and Shi'ites view the Islamic Holy Law very differently, but what we have today is a breakdown in all Islamic authority, especially among the Sunnis, which constitute approximately 86 percent of the Muslims in the world and who are most active in the jihadi movements everywhere.

The Sunnis do not have a religious hierarchy. As such, there are numerous Sunni authorities, or even self-proclaimed authorities who can and do issue *fatwas* at will to justify anything a particular government, organizations or groups such as the Islamic State (ISIS/IS), al-Qa'ida, the Nusra Front, the PLO, or Hamas, wish to do. There is no trouble finding a religious authority to issue its stamp of approval for anything their leaders wish to do. And rarely do we find Islamic religious leaders condemning the religious decisions other religious authorities issue. Do they remain silent because they agree with others'

13

fatwas or out of fear or retribution if they open their mouths? No one can know for sure what the answer is. Nevertheless, we can make an educated guess based on a combination of many factors. Certainly, fear is an important element. But in many instances, these Sunni religious authorities quickly agree, as can be deduced from the private conversations they have with people whom they trust.[9]

Unlike the Sunnis, the Shi'ites do have a recognized religious hierarchy, to which many Shi'ites look for guidance. But even here, the Shi'ite leaders at the top—*i.e.,* their Grand Ayatollahs—don't have a formal hierarchy. Each one is something like the Catholic Pope. They continuously jockey for domination against each other. Sadly, the traditional Shi'ite establishment has been destroyed by the Iranian government, which has politicized Shi'ism to such an extent that most of the Grand Ayatollahs reject the Iranian government's decisions but cannot say so publicly for fear of being imprisoned or assassinated by the Iranian regime. (More on the Shi'ites later.)

---

[9] We know from personal experience and conversations with long time associates of numbers of Sunni religious leaders. They can be quite direct in private, but fear saying such things in public, because they could be murdered by Muslims who do not agree with them.

THE SPREAD OF WAHHABISM

The vast majority of Islamic terrorism is Sunni. How do the governments in Sunni Muslim societies tackle Islamic jihadism that threatens to overthrow existing Sunni governments which the jihadis label "apostates?" A fascinating example is what happened in Saudi Arabia when what the Saudis would call "Islamic extremist jihadis" took control of the holy mosque in Mecca in 1979.[10] The Saudis follow a strict version of Sunni Islam—Wahhabism—which was itself an 18th century Islamic Reform Movement based on the already most strictly applied school of Sunni Islam—the Hanbali school of Islamic jurisprudence, "the strictest of the strict." But was it "strict enough?" To ISIS and al-Qa'ida, the Saudi government, supported by the Saudi Wahhabi religious establishment, are apostates. They allow Western influences into the kingdom, allow non-Muslims to live and work on Islam's most holy place on earth, and thus are serving the interests of the non-Muslims. They are therefore guilty of apostasy; the punishment for which in Islam is death. From ISIS, al-Qa'ida, and other extreme Muslim jihadi groups, the Saudis must be eliminated because they are Muslims.

How did these groups come into existence? In short, the Saudis themselves gave birth to them. In 1979, a group of jihadis took over the *ka'ba*, the holiest site in Islam, by force and refused to leave. These terrorists accused the Saudi government of not being committed enough to jihad, which is an essential part of Islam. This act deeply humiliated the Saudis in the eyes of the entire Muslim world. That is because the Saudis control Mecca and Medina and are responsible for protecting these sites. (The Saudi king is known as the "Guardian of the two most holy Muslim cities—Mecca and Medina.") These jihadis shamed the king and his government. As no weapons are allowed to be used in the holy mosque in Mecca, the government was in a quandary. The only way the Saudis could expel those who took over the mosque was by force, which is strictly forbidden in Islam. How could it end this siege without a *fatwa* from the Wahhabi religious establishment that using force was permissible?

---

[10] For details of this conundrum, see "The Siege of Mecca: The 1979 Uprising at Islam's Holiest Shrine," by Yaroslav Trofimov 9 September 2008. https://www.amazon.com/Siege-Mecca-Uprising-Islam's-Holiest/dp/0307277739/ref=sr_1_fkmr0_1?s=books&ie=UTF8&qid=1488586134&sr=8-1-fkmr0&keywords=surge+trofimov

The Wahhabi establishment itself was in a quandary because Islam requires jihad. How could the Wahhabi religious figures oppose jihad? After some effort, a legal fiction was devised. According to this agreement, the religious establishment issued a *fatwa* allowing the government to re-take the mosque by force. Moreover, the religious leadership agreed to the government decision to ban radical jihadi groups that might threaten the monarchy and which operate inside Saudi Arabia. But in return, the Saudis agreed that they would fund the export of jihad extensively everywhere outside the kingdom, and support the spread of Islam everywhere else in the world.[11]

Then, the Saudis began funding Wahhabi religious propaganda everywhere, which brought about the creation of most of the radical Islamic groups which terrorize the entire world today. The Saudis and other rich Wahhabis outside of Saudi Arabia—most notably in other Arab Gulf countries—injected massive amounts of money to spread their version of fanatical Wahhabi Islam. What is even more interesting is that some Gulf countries—most notably Qatar, which is also Wahhabi—began to compete with the Saudis as to whom could be more dedicated and zealous. They spread *da'wa* (the call to Islam, understood as prelude to jihad if not accepted) everywhere.

Places like Indonesia which historically had a much milder form of Islam became targets for the Wahhabis. The Indonesian Muslim leadership, for example, could not compete against the seemingly unlimited deep pockets of the Gulf Wahhabis. Young Indonesian Muslim men began to grow beards; their women began to cover their heads with the *hijab* (head scarf) or even *niqab* (face covering) in ways never seen before in Indonesia.

Penetration of Wahhabism into the Western World

Wahhabis became active not only throughout the Muslim world, but began to proselytize among the Muslims in Europe and North America. Wahhabis have since 1979 funded the building of the overwhelming majority of mosques in Canada and the U.S., and supplied Islamic teachers and religious leaders who spread their anti-Western, anti-non-Muslim, and anti-any other type of Islam but theirs throughout the Western hemisphere.

---

[11] Ibid.

16

Muslims have learned to use Western culture against itself. Some Muslims, when speaking to Western audiences, have gone out of their way to label Islam as a religion. While it definitely concerns itself with the relationship between God and mankind, it is actually more of a civilization which also involves politics and military activities. Historically, the *raison d'être* of a Muslim state has been to expand Islam, to conquer other lands for Islam, and to eventually take over the whole planet.

But since our authorities and intellectual leaders have labeled Islam a religion, we in the West have been reticent to interfere in Islamic activities. That has enabled the Muslim jihadi operatives to work quietly and patiently to create cadres of disgruntled young Muslims, right under our noses, who are extremely susceptible to the lure of jihad. Islamic mosques, Islamic Centers, religious events, their prayer services, and other activities have been placed off-limits to our police and FBI. Moreover, as some began to wake up to the possibility of homegrown terrorism springing up in our mist, our leaders have been uncomfortable about acting. We have embraced organizations like CAIR (Council on American Islamic Relations), the HAMAS branch in the U.S., which has its historical roots as a front for the Muslim Brotherhood, and was identified by the Department of Justice as an unindicted co-conspirator in the 2007 Holy Land Foundation HAMAS terror funding trial, the largest terror-funding case in U.S. history. Today CAIR remains one of the most active anti-Western jihadist organizations in the world. Too many of our leaders have invited these anti-Americans to the White House and other symbols of America in order to "prove" that Islam is a religion of peace.

President Obama's total unwillingness to label jihadi groups around the world as they label themselves ISLAMIC marked a major success for the stealth jihad operations of CAIR and other Muslim Brotherhood front groups in the U.S.

Given our own traditions, and because these mosques and activities are labeled religious, Americans and Europeans have had a natural reticence not to interfere with their activities.

Land was much less important than familial, clan, and tribal identity. Muhammad tried to create a super-structure based on these identities. Islam was like one big super-tribe, where people's responsibilities and liabilities are based on the tribal structures in which they grew up. Islam, as a result, views all Muslims as "brothers" or "sisters," responsible for each other and against the non-Muslims, whom it seems as one big "super-tribe" united against the non-Muslims. This concept helps us understand how Muslims worldwide, irrespective of nationality, language, or place where they live, feel a sense of solidarity with each other, unlike, for example, how Europeans Christians of different ethnic backgrounds felt towards each other.

That Islam was able to expand so quickly throughout the Middle East, North Africa, and Central Asia tells us much about those areas. It also shows how circumstances of history have enormous impact not only upon the people involved but for future generations to come.

Islam is, in essence, the victory of Arabian tribal society, with its values and mores, superimposed on the new religion it created, even though Islam incorporated much of the culture and structures that it encountered as it conquered the surrounding cultures

Muhammad and his followers existed at a time when the two great civilizations in that part of the world—the Byzantine Christian and the Persian Empires—were exhausted after having fought each other for the previous 25 years. As a result, they were unable to stand up against the onslaught of what amounted to desert tribes, upon whom they had always looked down. Both of these empires developed a highly sophisticated group of sayings, proverbs and curses to express their contempt for the Arabs.

Muhammad as a Tribal Warlord Ruler who Succeeds in Getting Disparate Elements to Work Together under Him (Called *Hakam* in Classical Arabic)

Muhammad's greatness as a leader derived from his ability to knit together disparate groups of people who constantly raided each other, to work together for a common goal—later to be termed Islam. Interestingly, when Muhammad died, many of these tribes who had developed personal ties with him, left the alliance he had built.[12] That this group of believers remained disunited was clear from the fact and many groups did not accept Abu Bakr, the man those around Muhammad chose as their leader (and first Caliph), and reverted back to their pre-Muhammad alliances, tribes, etc. As a result, Abu Bakr was forced to lead the first Great Islamic Reformation, as he fought the *Ridda* Wars, to force the wayward tribes back under the black flag of Islam.[13] This also expresses itself in the rampant violence which typified the post-Muhammad period until the founding of the Arab-Muslim Umayyad dynasty in Damascus. That period (631-660 CE) is filled with enormous unrest and bloodshed between both the Arabs and the peoples they encountered on their way out of Arabia to conquer what later became known as the Muslim world.

So how did the Arabs conquer the Byzantine Christian and the Persian Empires? In the early 600s, the Persians and Byzantines, both highly developed civilizations with great military institutions, fought each other mercilessly. Areas such as today's Syria, Lebanon, and Israel, beforehand part of the Byzantine Empire, became battlegrounds. In the process, these two great empires weakened each other to such an extent that they were simply not able to fight off the relatively small groups of Arab tribesmen coming out of the desert. For example, the Christian rulers of Jerusalem (which, since the Roman repression of the Bar Kokhba Jewish revolt from 132-135 CE, was renamed *Aeliya Capitolina,* then the name used in both the Christian chronicles and Arabic chronicles at that time, with the goal to de-Judaify that city after the Jewish revolt) describe the Arab conquest of Jerusalem as follows: "These tribes came out of the desert. As they approached Jerusalem, there were no forces to stand up against them, and so Jerusalem— undefended—simply gave in to them. These Christian chronicles had no idea who these tribesmen were. All the Christians knew was that they did not have the power to stand up against these desert Arabs. Moreover, in these chronicles, the desert nomads aren't called Muslims. (It's not clear from the historical record whether the words Muslim or Islam had even been invented yet.[14]) The chronicles say they called

---

[12] See the BBC Documentary Islam, The Untold Story. By Tom Howard: https://vimeo.com/79051482 https://www.youtube.com/watch?v=MZuNNkojDYg

[13] It is no mere coincidence that Abu Bakr al-Baghdadi chose this *nom de guerre* for himself, as he, too, has led a Great Islamic Reformation in the 21st century to purify the ranks of Islam once again.

[14] Ibid, Islam the Untold Story

themselves "believers." But in what? It appeared that they had not yet gotten their narrative straight. Jerusalem surrendered without a fight.

But the Arabs then moved on and did not attach much importance to that place. They eventually built and established their provincial capital in Ramlah (today's Ramle), a city due east of today's Tel Aviv, a city built on sand as the name describes. (In Arabic, the word for "sand" is "*raml*," which was more familiar to them than the urban civilizations in the northern part of the Middle East).

How can we describe the battles between these believers, who later called themselves Muslims, and others? Though some today would like to glorify these battles as major encounters between the Muslims and those they conquered, the chronicles of the time make it clear that these were small battles of raiding parties against locals, who as a result of the endless Byzantine-Persian battles, did not have the strength to stand up against these nomads.

But this understanding also creates a problem for Muslims, who, despite a few setbacks, were on the march, conquering much of the known world, until they were finally stopped in the late 1600s at the Gates of Vienna. Why did they then begin to lose territory? Why were they in retreat? After all, Allah, as they understood him, wanted the whole world to live under Islamic rule, ruled by a Caliph, and under the sharia—the Islamic Holy law. The question is, "What went wrong?" as the eminent historian Bernard Lewis entitled his book about Muslim decline. And were the Muslims supposed to reverse this? Muslims came up with different answers to these questions, and the results are the internal feuds the Muslims are having today with each other and their fury directed at both the non-Muslims living among them and the non-Muslim world which they do not yet control.

Letting Bygones be Bygones

Another major "gift" to the Muslims of pre-Islamic Arabian culture is the inability to put the past behind them. Arabs and Muslims in general know their history, or at least many of the myths they are taught from childhood. While, on one hand, being grounded in one's past is important in formulating identity, Arab Muslim myths, when not grounded in reality can make life difficult for those who believe them. Instead of the concept of justice that we have in the West, pre-Arabian culture had the concept of "balance" (*'adl*).

The camel, one of the most essential elements of Arabian desert culture, is the source of many things in Muslim culture. In this case, it was important that the two sacks which the camel carried on both sides of its body be in balance. If they were not, the camel could not walk correctly and would veer off to the side. This was called "*mayil*" in Arabic.[15] Human relations mirrored this '*adl/mayil* situation. Clans, tribes, etc., had to make sure that their relationships were always in balance. In practice, that meant that if someone killed—accidentally or otherwise—another person, his clan/tribe had to pay for this, not by money but by avenging the death. Anyone from the other social unit was fair game. The relationship between the social units was in "*mayil*," meaning out of balance. If that blotch on the honor of the tribe which had been aggrieved by the death/murder was not avenged, then that imbalance passed down to the next generation to avenge. As such, men understood that their social units' honor, the most important of their possessions, had to be avenged at all costs when the opportunity presented itself. That could come quickly, or remain waiting for vengeance for generations. In this context, people/men can know people outside their social groups (families, clans, etc.), but they remain soldiers in the social group's army, and as such find difficulties maintaining strong ties with people outside their social group. If a problem arises between clans, for example, the personal views of two friends from opposing clans do not matter. They must demonstrate group loyalty no matter what happens. Solidarity with the group must be maintained at all costs.

As such, Islam says that all Muslims are brothers. That means that if there is battle between Muslims and non-Muslims, Muslims are supposed to take the side of the Muslims against the non-Muslims.

Often situations arise in which one group of Muslims relies on the protection of a non-Muslim power. An example of this is the Sunni-ruled Arab countries on the northern coast of the Persian Gulf who had relied on America to support then against their arch-enemy Iran, until the Obama Administration abandoned them and made an agreement with their arch-enemy Iran. None of these Arab governments overtly aligned with America, because that would shame them in the eyes of their fellow Muslims. Just as none of these Sunni-ruled countries are prepared to publicly admit that they now have a temporary alliance with the Jewish State of Israel, against their Shi'ite enemy Iran. Muslims at least overtly

---

[15] "Note On the Bedouin Image of 'Adl as Justice", by Clinton Bailey, The Muslim World, April, 1976

maintained a sense of solidarity against the non-Muslim, even if in practice they did otherwise.

We see evidence of this Muslim vs. non-Muslim solidarity in other areas as well. The Muslims feel a sense of shame that the non-Muslim/Western world has been able to defeat and thereby humiliate them, as Muslims have been in retreat ever since they were defeated/routed at the gates of Vienna on September 11, 1683. (Even though Islam lost Spain in 1492, the Muslims still were advancing in other places until 1683.)

Losing territory heaps shame on the Muslims; it must be avenged. And this is much of the source of the what we see happening today in Europe and are witnessing here in the U.S. This inability to let bygones be bygones is inextricably tied in with honor/shame, and is the source of so much of the Muslim "terrorism" as we call it. But Muslims know this as classic Islamic warfare, which is why so many glorify in it.

We in the West, Russia, China, and India all share the same history. We have taken Islamic territory, which is "rightfully theirs." According to the Islamic doctrine of "Sacred Space," any land ever conquered or occupied by Islam becomes forever *waqf,* or land dedicated to Allah and the Muslim community in perpetuity. Both their culture and the Islamic doctrine derived from it demand that they take it back, and then continue the march onward to "Islamize the entire world."

We ignore this at our peril! There is no way to compromise on this, no matter how much our political and leaders may think otherwise. This unending battle will continue either until Muslims rule the entire world or the rest of the world utterly defeats Islam.

To be sure, there is a dispute among jihadi Muslims as to what comes first. Some believe that it is more important to rid the Islamic world of fake Islamic rulers which now lead most of the Islamic world. Others believe that they must now bring the jihad to the non-Muslim-ruled world. What we are witnessing, it seems, is that different Muslims are doing different things, and that they are trying to accomplish both missions at once.

Islam has no Pope, *i.e.*, no central authority to look to on all matters for guidance, what we are seeing today is a cacophony of *fatwas—i.e.,* religion decisions whose authors, whatever their religious training, to justify any and every act Muslims wish to engage in. Sadly, for the American and other foreign governments that passionately try to find some Muslim religious authority to "prove" that particular acts of terrorism are "against Islam," probably the vast majority of Muslims may or may not accept that authority's ruling because it is just as easy to find a religious figure to justify whatever someone wants to do.

What's the Islamic Strategy Here?

The Muslim jihadis have learned very well how to use Western culture against itself, and thereby weaken their enemies and promote Islam. Their general strategy can be summarized as *Whack A Mole*. Use any tool that works against their non-Muslim enemies. When one fails, put it on the back burner in case it might be useful again in the future.

Westerners—especially Americans—have long ago abandoned the study of history, and thus have almost no knowledge of the past. As a result, it is easy to fool them by bringing up things they have long forgotten about and re-use them over and over again, after they have vanished from our memory. Another way of describing this approach is to quote Barack Obama's mentor, Saul Alinsky, who stated: "Keep trying new things to keep the opposition off balance."

That beautifully summarizes the approaches of the forces of Islamic jihad. They never defend; they're always on offense. And when we muster either the fortitude or logical arguments to defeat them, we can be guaranteed that they will change course and chose a different method of attack. Our approach in response has almost always been to react at first as a deer caught in the headlights. We are stunned and go on the defensive, not realizing that this approach is useless. The best approach is to instantly present a strong offensive to obliterate their arguments. But that requires a deep sense of history and knowledge which, sadly, few Westerners still have.

We must admire their persistence. The Muslim world never gives in.

As the greatest historian of the Middle East, the centenarian Professor Bernard Lewis, wrote about Islam, "These two religions [Christendom and Islam], and as far as I am aware, no others in the world, believe that their truths are not only universal but also exclusive. They believe that they are the fortunate recipients of God's final message to humanity, which it is their duty not to keep selfishly to themselves like the Jews or the Hindus, but to bring to the rest of mankind, removing whatever barriers there may be in the way." But Christianity seems to have lost its confidence. It has all but abandoned this approach, has gone on the defensive, and seems to do everything it can to appease the Muslims. That leaves Islam now as the sole religion still trying to force its message on others, using any means possible, whether peaceful or violent.

What this tells us is that in order to combat militant Islam, we have no choice but to be prepared at all times to go on the offensive, whenever they present us with or whatever new problem/approach with which we must contend. Never defend; never explain. Our only alternative is to obliterate each new attack before the small fire turns into a forest fire and destroys the entire landscape. The Latin adage sums it up beautifully: *Si vis pacem, para bellum*: If you want peace, prepare for war.

But that can happen only when and if the West regains its confidence, and begins to believe in itself. And as most of the rest of the world wants a confident America as leader of the free world—whether it wants to or not—then America needs the leadership to meet this challenge. Otherwise, America's friends and allies, and for that matter many of its apparent adversaries, will have to turn their backs on America and make compromises demanded by the forces which do not share America's vision of democracy, freedom, and human rights for everyone, irrespective of nationality, ethnicity, or religion. America in the early years of the 21st century withdrew from its leadership role in the world, with consequences measured in chaos and uncertainty. During these years, the forces of Islamic jihad and sharia rose up again, unopposed in any concerted way. If these trends are not reversed, the world must look forward to the renewed scourge of Islamic conquest across the world.

Understanding How Islam Fights

The authoritative *hadiths* of Bukhari provide context for Muhammad's actions: "War is deceit," is a saying Bukhari attributes to Muhammad (52:269). Another says, "By Allah, and Allah willing, if I take an oath and later find something else better than that, then I do what is better and expiate my oath." (Bukhari: V7B67N427)

Treaties in Islam

Muhammad's Hudaybiyyah agreement with his enemies serves to this day as the model for Islamic treaties with Muslims and non-Muslims alike.

What can we learn from the early period of Islam and the life of Muhammad which can help us understand the nature of how agreements in the Muslim world work? The classical example is the Hudaybiyyah treaty that the Muslim prophet Muhammad made with the Quraysh tribe—his own tribe—which controlled Mecca. That agreement became the basis for Muslim agreements both with non-Muslims, and between Muslims themselves. The overwhelmingly majority of Muslim scholars and sources agree with this. As such, we can learn about Muslim intentions by studying this agreement—however it is labeled— (peace treaty, truce, etc.) in order to understand what we can expect when dealing with Muslim governments and organizations.

The facts of the agreement are as follows: Muhammad could not defeat his Quraysh enemies who constituted such a serious threat that had he not come to some arrangement with them; they could have destroyed Muhammad and his forces. Muhammad was very savvy, and understood that he had no alternative other than to find a way to stop the fight, so that he and his young religion/forces could survive.

He consequently agreed to a ten-year truce with his enemies. In classic Arabian fashion, he expected to use this time to regroup and find a way to resume the battle and defeat his enemies. That ten-year agreement ended two years later, when Muhammad saw that he was strong enough to defeat the Quraysh. He broke the treaty, resumed the fight and defeated his enemy. Was this trickery? Was this lying? Or was this just the normal way of doing business in Arabia at that time?

Muhammad and his new religion were weak at that time and could not stand up against the forces that opposed them.[16]

No matter how we label it, what is important is to understand that that was the norm at that time in Arabia, and Muhammad acted as was expected. And Islam, though we call it a religion, is actually based on Arabian pre-Islamic tribal culture, from which this new religion drew so much of its values and mores.

Interestingly, today's Bedouins (Arab nomads) who see themselves and their lives as perfect images of their prophet, have the answer to this problem. When there is a conflict between Islam law and tribal custom, tribal custom wins out.

So what does this tell us about how to understand agreement between opposing parties? Agreements are at best truces (or *hudnas*). In fact, they are means by which the weaker/defeated party licks its wounds, and waits for the opportunity to at first build up its strength, and then go on to vanquish its enemies. In that context, there are no final peace treaties. Everything is temporary until they can resume their battles and defeat their enemies.

That is why there cannot be a permanent peace in the Muslim world and why bygones can never be bygones. Muslims therefore live in permanent uncertainty.   They can never be sure that someone will not try to avenge a perceived slight which might have happened generations ago. Nothing is ever forgotten. Nothing is forgiven. And if this is how Muslims deal with each other internally, *i.e.*, among people whom they at least on paper consider to be "brothers in Islam," how all the more so is it when they deal with non-Muslims.

It behooves the West to think about and digest this view of the world, because it enables us to understand how the Muslims understand agreements with each other, and how they understand agreements they made with the outside world.

The following examples are useful to explain the Muslim concept of warfare and agreements.

The Oslo Process: *Hudna*, Not Peace

Arafat was deeply humiliated by the outcome of the 1982 Lebanon War, which resulted in the PLO (Palestinian Liberation Organization)

---

[16] See *The Life of Muhammad – A Translation of Ibn Ishaq's Sirat Rasul Allah, by A. Guillaume, Oxford University Press, 1955)* & The Encyclopedia of Islam, Vol. 9, p. 661.

being forced into exile in Tunisia. For all intents and purposes, Israel and the United States resurrected Arafat when they tried to persuade him to enter into what the West saw as a peace process with Israel. Arafat, in fact, could hardly believe his luck, as the Oslo Process afforded him the chance to return from oblivion.

We in the West saw these talks as the beginning of the end of conflict between the Israelis and the Arabs. As the signing ceremony and fanfare on the White House lawn indicated, America, and many Israelis choose to see this agreement as the dawn of a new age. But was it? And how did the Arabs—most notably the Palestinians—understand this?

The Arab leader who signed for the Palestinians was Yassir 'Arafat, the leader recognized by the world as THE Palestinian leader. Arafat, a devout Muslim with a keen sense of his culture, smiled to the world, and said all the things Westerners and so many Israelis wanted to hear him say... Or did he?

On May 10, 1994, in a speech Arafat gave after the White House signing, Arafat said as follows: "This agreement [the Oslo Accords], I am not considering it more than the agreement which had been signed between our Prophet Muhammad and Quraysh, and you remember the Caliph Omar had refused this agreement and considered it Sulha Dania [a despicable truce]. But Muhammad had accepted it and we are accepting now this [Oslo] peace accord."[17]

This may not sit well with so many of the Americans and Israelis who worked so hard for this agreement, and many did their best to deny that the recording was authentic, because it did not sit well with what people wanted to believe. But they too gave up after some time, when technical evidence demonstrated that the voice on the tape was indeed that of Arafat.

Palestinian School Texts & Media on the Destruction of Israel

According to the Oslo Accords, the Palestinians must stop incitement against Israel, although their media and school texts continue to be filled with blatant antisemitic and anti-Israeli material. But Arafat and his cohorts signed the Oslo Accords, according to which Arafat et al agreed to stop incitement.

---

[17] Audio recording of Arafat speech in Johannesburg, May 10, 1994,
http://palwatch.org/main.aspx?fi=157&doc_id=9401

What then is the meaning of these agreements and signatures? Hudaybiyyah is the answer: "We Muslims will do and say whatever we must in order to bring Israel back under Islamic rule." Everything is permitted in order to advance Islam.

Compare this to the Oslo Treaty—where they agreed to end incitement and, of course, did nothing of the sort.

How does Islam deal with non-Muslims and relations between the Muslims and the non-Muslims?

The short answer is that there is only one narrative ... the Muslim narrative. Christian, Jewish and other non-Muslim narratives are false and meaningless from a Muslim point of view. That is why there is nothing to talk about and nothing to discuss.

The idea that there could be more than one way of understanding an issue, besides theirs, is simply impossible. Moreover, even among Muslims, there is only one narrative, the individual's, which means they cannot even agree among themselves on how to disagree.

Why is this so? And how does this relate to the concept of Islamic warfare? In more than 52 years roaming the Muslim world, talking with thousands of people in their native languages, it has been next to impossible to get others to accept—not that their view is the only way of looking at a problem—that there is more than one narrative which must be considered, if two people, nations, or alliances, are to co-exist. When one tries to explain that the fact might be different, or maybe that others might see this differently, one gets the impression that they are culturally incapable of considering other points of view. When they hear another view, they usually answer that that view is wrong. And when one patiently explains why such a view might be based on a skewed perception of reality, they get angry and the consequences can often lead to violence.

Because their narrative is the only narrative, they cannot make peace—as we understand the word—with others. What they do have instead is forced co-existence, until one or the other is strong enough to impose his views on the others. As such there can never be true, longstanding peace with others as we understand the concept in the West.

A few simple stories illustrate this problem: The Ahmadiyah movement—an Islamic sub-group—arose in the Indian sub-continent in the 19th century and today has followers throughout the world. They number about 2-3 million to the best of our knowledge, the largest quantity of whom are in today's Pakistan. Ahmadis define themselves as Muslims. Their holy book is the Qur'an. But they deny one basic tenet of "normative Islam"—that being *jihad.* They believe that all people should get along, and that they should not use violence against others when confronted with problems. In Pakistan, they live in constant fear of their Sunni neighbors, who abuse their women and children and kill Ahmadi men. Their "crime" is that Sunnis do not see them as true Muslims. Sunnis see them as renegade apostates, with whom Sunnis cannot co-exist; they must be eliminated. The doctrinal definition of Islam, according to what the scholars of Islam have agreed upon in scholarly consensus (*ijma'*), cannot include the Ahmadis because they deny a basic tenet of Islam—*jihad.* A jihad against Muslims?

Maybe, from a Western point of view, but certainly not from theirs. There is only one Islamic narrative, which does not include the Ahmadis. Given the Sunni Islamic view, there is no way to compromise. The Ahmadis must be destroyed.

A 'Spy' in Iran?

Years ago, on a long bus ride through the Iranian dessert, my fellow passengers were intrigued by the fact that I was reading the Qur'an and spoke Persian. They understood that I was a foreigner, because, when I boarded the bus, that they heard me talking with the bus driver who had asked me where I was from, and heard me answer that I was an American. They assumed at first that I must have been a Christian. But after the bus started moving, I pulled out a copy of the Qur'an and began reading to myself. People were confused. How could I be reading the Qur'an and not be, or not have become a Muslim? My fellow travelers were curious, because almost no one in that remote area on the bus had met a Christian who read the Qur'an. They all crowded around and began to ask questions. Oh, they said, you are an American but you are a Muslim. "No", I answered. "I am an American, but not a Muslim." They were in shock. They had never heard of nor seen anything like that before. "Then why are you reading the Qur'an", they asked. I responded that I wanted to learn about Islam, but was not interested in becoming a Muslim. "You mean, you are reading the Qur'an and have not become a Muslim?", they responded. I said "yes." I appreciated the Qur'an, and thought it worth reading, in order to gain insight into Islam, but nothing more. They simply could not conceive this possible. "You mean you are reading the Qur'an and that does not make you want to become a Muslim?", they shot back. I said "yes." They simply looked at me in amazement, because for them, the Qur'an was from Allah; it is his word. There was no other way of understanding this book. For them, this is impossible. I said that I have my own religion, and it is not Islam. "You mean that reading the Qur'an has not convinced you to become a Muslim?," they asked. I said, "al-hamdu-lillah (an Arabic phrase used by all Muslims meaning "Praise the Lord"), and I not a Muslim." This shocked them even more. "You mean you believe in God, are reading the Qur'an, but are not a Muslim?"

At first, they were speechless, but then began talking among themselves, telling each other that this must mean that I was a spy. Now I realized I was in trouble. I responded that I loved Iran and Iranian culture and wanted to learn as much as I could about Iran. But try as I might, I could not get them to understand that their narrative was not the only narrative in the world, and that I was studying Iran and Islam so I could appreciate the greatness of Iran even more. I didn't realize that I was digging myself in even deeper, "proving" to them from their cultural point of view that I was indeed a spy. Realizing I was in trouble, when we arrived at the next small town on the way, I decided to get off the bus and find my way from there. They had their narrative and were culturally incapable of understanding that others had other points of view.

Does their inability to accept that there can be other narratives hold across the board? Do all Muslims think this way? No one can of course generalize about all of anything. But there is no doubt that the huge overwhelming majority of Muslims think this way, which of course has major ramifications for confronting Islamic jihadi terrorism.

Compromise is impossible between people who believe that their narrative is the only narrative and others who believe in "live and let live." One cannot convince those who refuse to accept others having different points of view via peaceful means. In this situation, there can at best be a truce, until those who know theirs is the only truth are strong enough to impose their will and views on those who do not agree with them—or those others succeed in ultimately defeating those not willing to live in peace and tolerance.

In short, as the great Professor Bernard Lewis often said, their view can be summed up as follows: "I'm right. You're wrong. Go to hell!"

Why Have Wars? The Western Concept of War vs. the Muslim Concept: Knowing How to Wait vs. Western Impatience

Westerners look to solve problems. Given the nature of Islam, Muslim civilization lives with unsolvable problems, which rear their heads from time to time. Muslims cannot solve problems which are so basic to our understanding of the world. That's because for Muslims, the concepts of honor and shame are paramount, a conviction which prevents compromise. These two concepts are central to Muslim civilizations, but in today's world, almost completely alien to the Western world. For Muslims, spreading Islam—and by any means necessary—is a basic tenet of Islam.

We in the West are impatient, and when we decide to solve a particular problem, we look to solve it immediately. We say "are you part of the solution or part of the problem." Muslim culture finds this alien. Problems don't necessarily need to be solved, and they don't need to be solved until such point in time when a particular party has the strength to solve the problem in their ideal way. Patience is one of the most prized concepts in the Middle East. One can lie in wait for years, decades or longer until he can rectify the wrong that has been done to him.

ONCE IT'S MUSLIM, IT'S ALWAYS MUSLIM

From an Islamic point of view, once a territory is conquered for Islam, it remains Islamic forever (in Arabic, *Futuh* means opening a new territory to Islamic domination). That means that Spain, Portugal, large parts of Russia, southeastern Europe, all of India, Xinjiang in China, and Israel, are in permanent danger of Islamic attacks. From a Muslim point of view, all of these territories belong to the Muslims forever and only Muslims have the right to rule these lands.

When Muslims lose control over such lands, Islam wages unending battles and uses any means available to rectify this offense against Allah. These lands must be returned to Muslim rule. That such lands are not now under Islamic control represents a blotch on Muslim honor, which must be avenged. Any agreement to do otherwise must be understood as temporary agreements at best (*hudnas* again), until the Muslims have the capabilities of returning these lands to Islamic rule within the Dar al-Islam.

Muslims know how to wait until the appropriate time has come, when the outside world is weak, and no longer has either the will or the ability to defend itself. Then, when the Muslims sense this weakness, they strike, which is the source of spreading unrest in Europe, which, as a post-Christian society, no longer has the will to stand up for its values and civilization.

We in the West might be very happy with ourselves by being able to point to this or that Islamic religious figure who castigates those whom we label terrorists, but those engaged in such activities could not care less about what our favorite mullah or 'moderate Muslim' might say. The point we of the West must understand is that Islamic doctrine commands all Muslims to fight or support jihad until the whole of the earth is conquered for Islam and subjugated to rule of sharia under a Caliphate. While some Muslims of every generation may choose not to participate in these obligations of their faith, there is no disagreement that these are, in fact, obligations of the faith and that those who hear and obey can justify their actions in the sacred scriptures of Islam.

ISLAM AND INTERNATIONAL LAW

We also pride ourselves in following "International law," which, in fact, is Western law. But do the Muslims recognize this law? Many Muslim leaders indeed do pay lip service to this law—when it specifically serves their interest to do so. But do Muslims recognize this law, or do they use it when they want to justify their actions and reject it when they choose to? The following story provides insight into how Muslims handle this law which is, in the end, not theirs:

> The Iranians held American diplomats hostage for 444 days from November 4, 1979—January 20, 1981. This was a violation of International law from a Western point of view. But Grand Ayatollah Khomeini—the leader of the Iranian Revolution—understood this differently. The eminent Egyptian journalist and editor Mohamed Hassanein Heikal was a close friend of Khomeini's. The Americans asked him to go to Iran and talk with Khomeini about releasing our hostages. Heikal agreed to do so and fly to Iran and went to Qom where Khomeini lived. The two of them spoke. After Heikal left Iran, he was interviewed by Ted Koppel of the ABC program 'Nightline' about the conversation he had with Khomeini. Heikal said that he mentioned to Khomeini that holding diplomats hostage was a violation of International Law. Khomeini looked at Heikal and said: "Is this International Law

Muslim? Heikal answered "No." Khomeini went on: "Were Muslims involved in creating this law?" Again Heikal answered "no." Khomeini then said: Then there is no International Law.

About ten years later, in 1990, when the head-of-state membership of the Organization of Islamic Cooperation (OIC—now numbering 57 members) met in Cairo in 1990, they jointly rejected the UN Universal Declaration of Human Rights and established the Cairo Declaration in its stead.[18]

For Muslims, Allah's law is the sharia, and it must be the law of the world—not that all Muslims agree on what the sharia is, and how to implement it. But significant number of Muslim leaders—most assuredly Recep Tayyip Erdoğan of Turkey—look forward to the day that the sharia will be the law their countries, and eventually the entire world.

So how to square the circle? How can Muslim leaders avoid saying they do not recognize International Law? Again, two stories from the above-mentioned hostage crisis are illustrative:

Mansour Farhang, an Iranian who had taught at Princeton University, left that university and became Iran's UN ambassador under Khomeini. Farhang was very well-versed in the ways of the West, and, in typical Iranian fashion, knew how to lull the West into passivity, which almost assuredly was a major reason the Iranians chose him for the job.

One evening, Ted Koppel interviewed him and an Iraqi representative on "*Nightline*" when Iraq invaded Iran in 1980. Farhang said that the Iraqi invasion of Iran was a violation of International Law. Koppel shot back, "How dare you cite International Law! You have been holding our diplomats hostage which is a serious violation of International Law." Not missing a heart-beat, Farhang responded: "They are our **guests**!"

---

[18] The Cairo Declaration on Human Rights in Islam was formally presented to the UN General Assembly three years later, in 1993, and accepted. Articles 24 and 25 are as follows: ARTICLE 24: All the rights and freedoms stipulated in this Declaration are subject to the Islamic Shari'ah. ARTICLE 25: The Islamic Shari'ah is the only source of reference for the explanation or clarification of any of the articles of this Declaration.http://hrlibrary.umn.edu/instree/cairodeclaration.html

SOLVING AND ADDRESSING PROBLEMS: MARITAL ALLIANCES AND ...

Traditionally, in Muslim society, problems were often solved through marriage alliances. Families married off their daughters to sons of the opposing families in order mitigate problems.

For example, the former foreign minister of Iraq, Khoshyar Zebari, a Kurd from the Kurdistan Region of Iraq, was the product of an interesting alliance. The Barzanis and the Zebaris had been at each others' throats for eons, with much blood spilled between them.

In order to stop this bloodshed, the legendary Kurdish leader Mullah Mustapha Barzani's sister was married off to Mahmud Agha Zebari, one of the leaders of the Zebari clan. They had a son named Khoshyar.

Khoshyar Zebari — the product of a marriage between the Barzani and Zebari families — served as a loyal member then of Barzani's entourage both in Washington and later as Iraq's Foreign Minister. That's how long-term animosities can be solved. (Khoshyar is also the uncle of the present leader of the Kurdistan Regional government in today's northern Iraq.)

Forms of Islamic Warfare

Since the advent of Islam, Muslims have used whatever means possible to achieve their goals of spreading Islam throughout the world. These have included warfare, economic coercion, and sending out preachers to convince the locals. In short, anything that works, Muslim use.

Agreements made between most Muslims and non-Muslims, whether they be political, military, or otherwise, are understood as part of the strategy of Islamifying the whole world. There can be no true dialogue between religions. If there appears to be one, it has been almost always used as a means to explain Islam to the non-Muslims, and eventually get them to convert to Islam. Time is never a problem, because Middle Eastern culture, from which Islam emanates, values patience. Everything comes in time. Use every means possible to advance the cause. Always be on the offensive. Never be only on the defensive. Never admit failure. Never admit that you are wrong. When you are losing, always blame the other for your failures. Use history—real or invented—to prove your points. And when dealing with the West, which has almost totally lost its way and doesn't know history, make up any stories you need to in order to intimidate your adversaries or counterparts into giving in.

Practically, that means that whatever the latest ideas or philosophies that are in vogue today are the ones that Islam uses. That usually puts Westerners on the defensive, forcing the Westerners who mostly just want to get along, to try and find ways to defuse the wrath of their Muslim political, military, and religious counterparts. In short, Muslims have historically used any method they can to advance Islam, and have had no problem getting some religious authority to issue a *fatwa*—a religious decision—approving whatever they wish to do.

The following examples illustrate how this process works today.

On Turkey's Erdoğan—Say and Do Whatever You Need to Do to Advance Islam.

1. *Erdoğan on the Jews & the Muslim prophet Muhammad*

Turkish President Erdoğan was once asked what the Jews of Turkey think of him. Erdoğan smiled and said that they love him, just like the Jews loved Muhammad. To the untrained ear, this sounds plausible, except that Erdoğan assumed that the questioner knew nothing about the relationship between Muhammad and the Jews. Given Erdoğan's experience, he knew that answer should suffice to silence the questioner. But this was not the case. Erdoğan did not realize that the questioner was an expert on early Islam and knew that Muhammad and his cohorts murdered many of the Jews of Medina when they refused to convert to Islam. What happened was that Muhammad wanted the three Jewish tribes of Medina, one of which was very powerful, to recognize him as a prophet, and then to convert to Islam. When they refused, Muhammad, a very charismatic leader, formed an alliance with the non-Jewish tribes of Medina and defeated the Jews. At the very moment his generals decapitated the leader of the largest Jewish tribe, Muhammad raped that leader's wife, Safiya, whom Muslims say loved Muhammad, converted to Islam, and became his wife.

With time, it became clear that Jews could live under Islam, as long as they knew their place—*i.e.,* as politically and socially inferior people. This status, later granted also to Christians, is called "dhimmitude."

So did the Jews love Muhammad? Hardly. They refused to accept him as a prophet and never revolted against Islamic rule, because the consequences would have been dire. So much for the Jews loving Muhammad, and so much for Erdoğan's claim. Erdoğan had expected to silence the questioner, but blew up when the questioner explained the relationship between Muhammad and the Jews. Erdoğan had been "outed." In anger, Erdoğan, lashed out at the questioner, attacking him personally, and then moved on to the next questioner.

2. *Erdoğan and his former close friend former President Obama*

Similarly, Erdoğan relishes intimidating others, and making them submit to his dictates. President Obama, for example, in the early part of his first term in office, called Erdoğan the leader he most admired and respected in the world. How did Erdoğan return the compliment? By working with the Islamic State in Iraq and al-Sham (ISIS) and Muslim jihadi fighters against American interests, all the while pretending that he was an ally of the U.S. Obama continued to support Erdoğan, even after it became publicly known that Turkey's government was looking the other way when ISIS and other Islamic jihadis were using Turkey as a way to get in and out of Syria and Iraq, and selling oil via Turkey on the international market.[19]

Was Erdoğan spitting in the face of President Obama? How did the Americans in charge of foreign affairs understand what Turkey was doing with ISIS *et al*? They at first chose to ignore the reality. They reacted as the great historian Bernard Lewis often described the foreign policy establishment in the U.S. "I spit in your eye and you say it is raining."

What can we learn from the above? These two stories illustrate how, from the very beginning Erdoğan was prepared to use any means to neutralize his enemies and advance the cause of Islam. Erdoğan saw what ISIS, the Muslim Brotherhood, and other jihadi organizations were doing as ways to advance his goal of neutralizing his opponents and advancing the cause of Islamifying the world.

Instead of addressing the issues, so many of our foreign policy establishment made "*ad hominem*" attacks against those who argued that Erdoğan, even well before he became Prime Minister, supported ther Muslim Brotherhood. Erdoğan's ultimate goal was to destroy the democratic and secular Republic that Turkey's founder, Mustafa Kemal Atatürk, had created in the 1920s.

Erdoğan told us straight-forwardly what he thought about democracy. He said that democracy was like a train: when you reach your destination, you get off.[20] We in the West chose to ignore this at our peril.

---

[19] Sanger, David E. and Julie Hirschfeld Davis, "Struggling to Starve ISIS of Oil Revenue, U.S. Seeks Assistance From Turkey," September 13, 2014.
https://www.nytimes.com/2014/09/14/world/middleeast/struggling-to-starve-isis-of-oil-revenue-us-seeks-assistance-from-turkey.html

[20] This quote has appeared in many places. One is: http://www.economist.com/news/special-report/21689877-mr-erdogans-commitment-democracy-seems-be-fading-getting-train

3. Erdoğan and European leaders

The Turks were stopped in their advance into Europe on September 11, 1683, at the gates of Vienna. From then on, they lost one battle after another until they were forced to withdraw to their present borders which were finalized about a century ago. Atatürk, the founder of modern Turkey, said that Turkey had no claims on any territory outside of Turkey, and that the borders of the Turkish Republic were sacrosanct. Erdoğan thinks differently. As a devout Muslim, he "knows" that all the territory between the Turkish border and Vienna is Muslim, and must be reconquered for Islam, because all territory conquered by Islam remains Islamic forever. But how to reconquer this land and continue the march into Europe, which the Turks had to abandon in 1683? Any method is acceptable. First of all, flood the area with Muslims, which is exactly what he has been doing for the past few years. But these Muslims naturally moved northward beyond Vienna into Germany and beyond, hastening the day when these areas beyond Vienna also come under Muslim rule. He knows that traditionally, Muslims in Europe have stayed to themselves and not made problems for the leaders of the country in which they live, until they reach a critical mass. Then, the Muslims make demands. At first, they take over neighborhoods. The police—often afraid to enter these areas—gradually withdraw. Most often, these neighborhoods then became little "Islamistans" (Islamic enclaves, or "No Go Zones," which gradually expand, as their population increases and takes over nearby areas). Gradually in these areas, Islamic law in some form becomes the norm.

Many European leaders—especially those in Western Europe—feel guilty about the genocide they and their fathers committed against the Jews and others during World War II, and, as a result no longer believe in themselves or their own traditional civilizational values. The more the Muslims assert themselves, the more the European leaders try to bargain with the Muslims to make sure the Muslims keep to themselves. Erdoğan has put them in a "damned if they do, damned if they don't" situation. If these leaders don't "bribe" him by paying for refugee camps and food for Muslims coming from Syria, Afghanistan, Iraq, and beyond, then Erdoğan threatens to unleash them on Europe. But if he agrees to stem the refugee tide, then in return, he demands that the Europeans abolish the need for visas for all Turkish citizens, allowing Turks—some 75 million strong—to travel and stay in Europe. Either way, either by letting the refugees in or by letting in Turkish citizens, who are 99% Muslim, Europe becomes "Islamified," and the march of Islam again resumes beyond the Muslim defeat at Vienna in 1683. And the day that Europe is taken over by the Muslim and becomes part of the Muslim world comes closer. So this is a win-win situation for Erdoğan and the Muslims and a loss for post-Christian Europe.

Immigration

One of the most interesting and important weapons of Islamic warfare today is immigration. This is particularly important for Europe, but is also becoming more so in the U.S., Canada, and other places as well.

If we don't want to face what Europe is going through, it would behoove us to examine what is going on there with the Muslims in the U.S. and Canada, develop strategies to confront these problems, and find appropriate tactics within our own culture to ensure that we do not face the threat of the imposition of sharia on the U.S. and Canada.

Before we address this issue, it is important to realize that there is no central office or government in the Muslim world coordinating the attempt to take over the non-Muslim world. It is simply such an important part of Islam that it has become a central element of the Muslim cultural DNA.

One of the ways that Muslims are in the process of taking over Europe—at least from their point of view—is taking over from inside. How Muslims living in both Germany and France have reacted to what they deem their "host countries" and the citizens of these countries is instructive.

When Muslims come and settle in a new place, taking over and imposing sharia on the whole area is not, for most of them, their most important immediate goal. By and large, like most immigrants everywhere, they are most concerned about settling in, getting jobs, and making new lives for themselves in their new domains. During this stage, those non-Muslims among whom they live don't see them as a threat, because the Muslims most often stay to themselves and rarely deal with the locals, except with needed.

As they settle in, one of the most important things they do in the beginning is set up prayer rooms, in order to address their spiritual and cultural needs. These prayer rooms eventually turn into small, often inconspicuous mosques. But as more and more Muslims join them, they begin to build formal mosques, which usually still do not impinge upon their non-Muslim neighbors, culturally or otherwise. At this stage, everything seems relatively innocuous. In Germany, for example, German Christians often, at this stage, complain about the music they play, or the smell of the food they prepare. Nothing more serious than that usually arises.

But as these Muslim communities grow and develop their own communal infrastructure, they begin to make demands upon their neighbors, the local schools, and the police. Many of these demands seem innocuous at first because they seem so reasonable. In Germany, for example, there is a law according to which, when there is a particular number of people from a specific faith, those people have the right to ask for religious instruction in school, which is paid for by the German government. Moreover, this law requires that the people themselves chose the religious instructor, and that the government has no right to intervene in their choice. In the 1980s, for example, when the number of Muslims reached that critical mass in particular neighborhoods, the Muslims asked for religious instructors. The Turkish government at that time, still strongly Atatürkist and secular, realized that the religious teachers, if not under supervision, could preach radical Islamist views. Turkey itself had to face that problem, and its government had developed a curriculum, produced books, and trained Turkish teachers to teach Islam in a way which was not political and did not call for the control of the state. The Turkish authorities went to their German counterparts and asked the German government if they could supply textbooks and teachers to teach non-political Islam—more based on morals and values—to the young Turkish Muslims in German schools.

The German authorities refused the Turkish government's request because according to German law, governments are not allowed to interfere with religious training. The Turkish government politely warned them that the Germans, if they did not try to control what type of Islam was taught to their Muslim youth, would eventually suffer serious consequences. The Germans made it clear that they could not accede to Turkish government requests because of the German law's requirement that there be a total separation of religion from the state.

The Wahhabis and the Libyans, both cognoscente of the German law, set up foundations—seemingly unconnected to the Saudi, Libyan, and other Persian Gulf countries—which taught their form of Islam, which, given its loathing of Western society, guaranteed that there would be a whole new generation of Muslims in Germany who were being trained to eventually take over German culture, and impose Islam and its holy law on Germany.

The Saudis, Libyans, and other Gulf states brought in viciously anti-Christian, anti-Western and anti-German teachers and religious functionaries who preached jihadi Islam. All this was happening under the eyes of the German government, which was powerless to intervene, because this was "religion" and they were therefore forbidden to get involved in any way with religious instruction and activities.

The result has been that a young generation of Turkish Muslims living in Germany, educated in Germany, yet at the same time being indoctrinated by jihadist Islamic preachers, has different ideas from those of their parents, and, because of their increasing numbers, want to impose their Islamic views on Germany society.

During the 1980s and 1990s, as this process was in full bloom, it was interesting to listen to German government officials who would tell us that Muslims were welcome in Germany as long as they accepted German culture and moral values. Women in Germany, for example, were understood to be equal to men and were not controlled by the men in their lives. When we questioned the German authorities as to what they might do when/if they saw that the Turkish Muslims living in Germany did not accept these German values, the Germans were at a loss for words.

Today, given Germany's sad past regarding non-Christian Germans and other non-German Christians, the German government has welcomed over 1,000,000 Muslims from the Muslim world into their territory for economic reasons, but who have no intention of assimilating into German culture, and are already finding ways to impose their Muslim values on Germany society.

In this context, we should note what is happening to German non-Muslim women who now feel uncomfortable and threatened walking in their streets because immigrant Muslims and their multiplying descendants there have values which often threaten these women.

Any woman, for example, who does not cover up her shoulders and wear a headscarf is advertising her "availability" because in the societies from which these immigrants came, such a woman does "immoral" things. Indeed, the Qur'an itself warns women to cover lest they be 'molested' (that is, raped, by Muslim men, who understand Islamic clothing to indicate a woman who is 'off-limits,' while all others are 'fair game').[21]

---

[21] See Qur'an 33;59

At the same time, a young Muslim generation has come of age in Germany, many of whom have been taught similar values to those of the new immigrants. So, a merging takes place here.

As such we now see situations where entire neighborhoods in Berlin, for example, are becoming "no-go" zones for German police. The locals are imposing sharia on their neighborhoods while the German authorities stand aside and look in horror at what is happening in their society.

Do all "Muslims of Germany" ascribe to a faithful or devout Islamic lifestyle? Of course not, but they seem to be the minority, because either they will not, or they cannot, stand up and oppose what their more observant fellow Muslims are doing. These Muslims, who are doing their best to live in German society, simply live in fear of their more radical counterparts and are afraid to open their mouths, because they fear they would suffer serious consequences.

This is also the case in other European cities and countries outside Germany. Malmo, Sweden, for example, used to be a largely homogenous Swedish city with close ties to Copenhagen, directly across the channel. But today, as a result of Muslim immigration, native Swedes are abandoning that city. The police do not go into Muslim neighborhoods, and sharia is slowly but most definitely becoming the law of the land in Malmo.

In France, where North African Arab and Berber Muslims, and sub-Saharan black Muslims dominate, the same process is occurring. Many of the suburbs of Paris, (called *banlieux)* for example, are almost exclusively Muslim. No French, (post) Christian or otherwise, would risk entering these areas, and the French government often has little idea what is happening there. To be sure, these cities and towns are formally part of France, but all one has to do is to enter these areas to instantly feel that he has crossed the border into a foreign country. French law no longer applies in these places, and the police and other government agencies fear entering these areas.

As the great French historian Emmanuel Le Roy Ladurie once said at the conference on Muslim history, there are three types of Muslims in France:

1. French Muslims (*i.e.,* culturally French but of the Muslim faith);

2. Muslims of France (Muslims from other places being brought up in France and also respectful of family values, but deeply steeped in Islam);

3. Muslims living in France (*i.e.,* people physically but coincidentally living in France but living in Muslim enclaves and having no connection with French society or culture whatsoever).

What Ladurie worried about, with obvious justification, is that French Muslims (#1) were becoming Muslims of France (#2), and that Muslims of France (#2) were becoming Muslims living in France (#3). Ladurie said this in the 1990s, and sadly, his prediction is coming true.

France, in the past a militantly secular society where religious activity of any sort was legally discouraged in public, is now going by the wayside. On Friday, it is now common to see Muslims praying publicly *en masse* in the streets, in areas traditional French people believe is their own.

Source: http://admin.americanthinker.com/images/bucket/2015-10/195469_5_.jpg

But they seem either powerless or unwilling to do anything to stop this activity.

Demographically, although the Muslim birthrate has decreased in Europe, it is still much higher than among traditional French, German, or other Western European populations. If current demographic trends continue—and there is no reason to think that they will not—then by the mid- and latter part of the 21st century, Europe will almost assuredly be part of the Dar al-Islam.

Can this be stopped? An Italian journalist phoned Bernard Lewis some years ago and asked that question. Prof. Lewis responded that the solution is for Europeans to start having more babies. The journalist did not want to hear this answer, and promptly hung up the phone on him. What did Prof. Lewis mean here?

Bernard Lewis

Once Europe stopped feeling confident about its culture, it stopped being religious, its churches were left empty, and its people begin to occupy themselves more with their heathenistic concerns rather than the values their ancestors held dear; they also stopped having children because children are both an economic drain and cramp their style.

Two instances come to mind. An American friend and his wife (both WASPs) vacationed last year in France with their baby son. As they walked down the streets of Paris, French citizens came up to them and were so excited to see a young French child. When these French realized that the couple and their children weren't French, they were notably disappointed. French children—descended of Frenchmen whose ancestors lived in France before the Islamic immigration, are often childless.

An Italian lecturer visiting an American university gave a lecture of the Muslim immigration to Italy coming to Lampedusa (an Italian island off the Libyan coast). He was happy about the North African immigration because he claimed that North Africans were among the smartest Muslims. He argued that Italy, because of its catastrophic demographic problems, should bring North Africans to Italy, and train them as doctors and nurses. When a questioner asked why, he said simply that these doctors and nurses could take care of the Italians as they reached old age. When the questioner responded that what he was arguing for would spell the end of Italian and European culture in Italy, the lecturer, without batting an eye, said, "What else can we do?"

Twice the Ottoman Turks were stopped at Vienna. First in 1521, and then again in 1683. From then on, a confident and powerful Europe pushed the Ottoman Muslims back to the present day borders of

European Turkey. Christian Spain also pushed the Muslims out of Spain in 1492. responded, "What else can we do? We are doomed."

These demographic trends, in short, illustrate the process of why post-Christian Europe seems doomed. Muslims, on the other hand, are overwhelmingly very confident about their future, and, if something drastic does not occur, can likely look forward to the end of European civilization, which will be taken over by Muslims.

But the Muslims never gave up. Today, a confident Islam, with no central body directing it, has now resumed its march in Europe, going around Vienna, and ignoring the Pyrenees, on its march to finally turn Europe from Dar al-Harb into Dar al-Islam. And from a Muslim point of view, once Islam rules these places, they shall remain under Muslim control forever.

America, Canada, Russia, China and beyond, be warned. Islam will use whatever methods it needs to, to bring its civilization to our shores/lands, and it will use every means possible, be they military, proselytizing, or cajoling us into submission. Islam thereby intends to become the dominant force in these lands, unless these countries study what has happened in Europe, develop strategies, and implement them to prevent the Muslims from conquering these nations, using whatever means they have at their deposal to do to us, what they are doing to Europe.

Almost all Muslims know this, and, even though there are many Muslims who do not see this as their most important goal in life, so many do, that it is important that we understand what is happening here and how to combat it, if we have the guts to do so.

The Invention of 'Islamophobia'

Another useful tool in the Islamic arsenal is Islamophobia. It was invented to intimidate people who question the policies of the self-appointed Islamic leaders in the U.S. and abroad. Its goal is to put people who oppose the march of Islam in Dar al-Harb on the offensive. Given the West's obsession with political correctness, few are willing to stand up and risk being labeled anti-anything.

This is particularly true of people who oppose the Sunni Salafis—whether ISIS, al-Qa'ida, the Muslim Brotherhood, CAIR (Council on American Islamic Relations, ISNA, the Holy Land Foundation, or other Islamic organizations whose sharia supremacist agenda stands in stark opposition to the U.S.'s Constitutional system.

If these organizations stated publicly what they are privately advocating, they would lose much of the support they have garnered from naïve Westerners. This absurdity has become so clear because American government leaders who deal with Muslim issues have become obsessed with defining who is and who is not a "true Muslim." The definition U.S. government leaders have used—even long before Barack Obama became President—presupposes that the only true Muslim is one who doesn't believe in American values.

When Muslim Americans—such as Zuhdi Jasser, President of the American Islamic Forum for Democracy, or writers such as Khaled abu Toameh of the Gatestone Institute—criticize their fellow Muslims for supporting terrorists and anti-freedom and democracy advocates both in the Muslim world and in the West, the Muslim organizations anointed by the State Department and the media are enraged. Over the years, we have heard senior officials and others in charge of Muslim affairs in the government and elsewhere charge that Jasser and abu Toameh and their likes are "not true Muslims." Who are these American officials and intellectuals to decide who is and who is not a true Muslim? Why do these officials and intellectuals succumb to charges of Islamophobia so easily? The leaders of organizations like MESA (The Middle East Studies Association), the largest international organization of academics who study/write about the Middle East, are also very quick to label those who do not buy their arguments as Islamophobic. And when they discuss organizations like Ahl al-Quran (Qurani'een) and scholars like Tawfik Hamid who reinterpret Islamic sources in ways that call for co-existence with the non-Muslims—not dominate them—these organizations and their like belittle them, saying they are not serious Muslims, or that they are lackeys of some country or government.

Is it not possible for Muslims to want to get along with, and even admire the Western principles or equality, democracy, women's rights, and getting along with others on an equal basis? The underlying message that the above-mentioned anointed groups and foreign leaders seem to be peddling is "no, they cannot be good Muslims" and loyal to the U.S. Constitution at the same time, because the definition of "Muslim" is "one who submits"—to the alien, hostile legal system known as sharia.

Are Muslims who want to find sources in Islam which accept the Western concepts of tolerance of others, and equality, and democracy "Islamophobic"?

So the label Islamophobia is just one more weapon in the Islamic arsenal to silence debate of what is happening throughout the Muslim world regarding non-Muslims, the non-Muslim world, and those who oppose the march of Islam throughout the world.

Islamic Warfare —the Shi'ite Perspective

The government of the Islamic Republic of Iran claims to be the authority for Shi'ite Islam.[22] How does the Iranian constitution address jihad and the spread of Islam throughout the world? That constitution defines the Islamic Revolutionary Guard Corps (IRGC) this way:

An Ideological Army

In the formation and equipping of the country's defence forces, due attention must be paid to faith and ideology as the basic criteria. Accordingly, the Army of the Islamic Republic of Iran and the Islamic Revolutionary Guards Corps are to be organized in conformity with this goal, and they will be responsible not only for guarding and preserving the frontiers of the country, but also for fulfilling the ideological mission of jihad in God's way; that is, extending the sovereignty of God's law throughout the world (this is in accordance with the Koranic verse *"Prepare against them whatever force you are able to muster, and strings of horses, striking fear into the enemy of God and your enemy, and others besides them"* [8:60]).

in accordance with the noble Qur'anic verse:

(Prepare against them whatever force you are able to muster, and horses ready for battle, striking fear into God's enemy and your enemy, and others beyond them unknown to you but known to God ... [8:60]).[23]

So it is clear that not only Sunnis see themselves in an eternal battle against the non-Muslim world, but so do the Shi'ites do as well, especially the self-appointed spokesmen for the Shi'ite world—i.e., the government of the Islamic Republic of Iran.

---

[22] "Shi'ites outside of Iran—especially in Iraq and the Persian Gulf—do not usually agree that the Iranian government represents them. But Iran is the largest and most powerful Shi'ite government, so it often forces Shi'ites in other parts of the world to remain silent, when they disagree with Iran."

[23] https://faculty.unlv.edu/pwerth/Const-Iran(abridge).pdf

As stated above, many Muslims are prepared to use any means available to bring Islam to the non-Muslims in whatever way works. It is therefore not surprising that when the Soviet Union was collapsing, the then-Supreme ruler of Shi'ite Iran, Ayatollah Ruhollah Khomeini, suggested that then-Soviet President Mikhail Gorbachev and the Soviet peoples consider Islam as an alternative to communist ideology [24]

The Arab-Israeli Conflict—in Islamic Context

If the Arab Muslims understood the Arab-Israeli conflict in terms of geography, borders, and nationalism, then the conflict would be solvable. Ways could be found to take into account the needs of the peoples involved and both sides could reach a final peace settlement. But that, unfortunately, is not how the Arabs understand the conflict, irrespective of whatever claims they make to tempt Western leaders and well-meaning Israelis to think otherwise. Unfortunately, the only framework which makes sense for understanding this conflict is an Islamic framework.

Despite what many Israeli leaders, intellectuals, and media may wish to believe, the conflict between Israel and the Arab world is—for better or worse—a conflict between Islamic civilization and the Jews. If Israel were weak, there would be no more Israel. If the Arabs were prepared to sign a final peace agreement with Israel, there would be peace between Israel and its neighbors.

Westerners—including the Israelis—have great difficulty understanding that whatever they dream up, they cannot solve the Arab-Israeli conflict. Almost every new American President and Secretary of State seems to believe that he/she will be the one to find that solution. Why did they always fail? Could it be that the reason is because of how Islam views Israel, whatever the size of the territory it controls?

When then-Syrian President Hafiz al-Assad once declared that "the very existence of Israel was an aggression," was he, in an Islamic context, correct?

Given how Islam views territory captured by Islam, there is no way to solve this problem until there is a radical thought revolution in Islam, which, for the foreseeable future, does not seem likely to happen.

---

[24] *The Greatest Jihād: Combat with the Self.* Alhoda UK. 2003. pp. 15-. ISBN 978-964-335-557-9.

The 1949 Rhodes Armistice Agreements Between the Israelis and the Arabs and the Aftermath

After the 1948 war between Israel and its Arab neighbors, the combatants sat down together at a United Nations-sponsored conference to deal with the results of the 1948 war. From a Muslim point of view, the results of the war could not have been worse. The Jews managed to fend off five Arab armies despite the Arabs' superior numbers and weaponry.

From a Muslim point of view, how could this have happened? In the Muslim lands, Christians and Jews had the status of Dhimmis—*i.e.,* protected peoples who, as long as they remembered their 2nd class place in society, were allowed to live under Muslim rule. These lands were Muslim, and had to be ruled by Muslims.

Allah, according to the sharia, had rejected the Jews and Christians. That's why Islam had been able to conquer so much of the world. And Allah had decreed that any land conquered by the Muslims must remain under Muslim rule forever.

So how could the Muslim Arabs sign a final peace agreement with the Jews who had conquered land that had been part of the Muslim world since 637 CE? Doing so would have violated a basic principle of Islam and humiliated the Muslim rulers in the eyes of their fellow Muslims. Both had to be avoided at all costs.

It was the Arabs, consequently, who insisted that the agreements be called Armistice Agreements—not Peace Agreements—emphasizing that these borders were temporary ceasefire lines—not permanent borders. In fact, the only borders recognized in these agreements were the former international borders of Egypt and Lebanon which British-mandated Palestine—which was not British sovereign territory—shared with those two countries. The other agreed-upon lines, were ceasefire lines, and were to be understood as such. The non-Muslim Jewish entity, therefore had no recognized borders with Jordan, which took over what many today refer to as the West Bank, and, with the then-Egyptian-held Gaza strip, which also had been part of pre-1948 British-mandated Palestine.

The Arab insistence on not recognizing Israel as having the right to live in peace with final internationally-recognized borders can only be understood in the context of Islam. After all, during the previous decade, the world had just experienced the death and destruction of World War II, and many other conflicts. Many people were displaced and many people lost their lives. In every case besides the Arab-Israel conflict, after these wars ended, Peace Agreements were signed, and new borders were recognized.

For the Muslim Arabs, the battle with Israel did not end in 1949. It could not have ended, because that would have meant that the Muslims would have recognized Jewish Israel's right to what they knew was sharia-mandated Islamic territory. No faithful or self-respecting Muslim could have done that.

That also explains why the Arabs have kept the refugees from British-mandated Palestine in refugee camps ever since then, and have not allowed them to become full citizens of the countries to which they fled.

Interestingly, there were many conflicts between Muslim countries throughout history which resulted in massive population shifts and displacement. In almost every instance, the Muslims were absorbed into the new political entities where they had fled within a short period of time. But this was not to be the case regarding the Arab Muslim states' conflict with Israel. With the possible exception of Jordan, Syria, Lebanon, and Egypt insisted on keeping the refugees in camps and not integrated into the societies to which they had fled. To the Western ear, this might sound insensitive at best, or even downright inhumane.

Understood in Islamic terms, however, the answer is simple. The refugees constituted and still constitute a weapon of Islamic warfare directed against the Jews who wrongly control Israel, which is and will remain forever, part of the Muslim world. Compassion takes a step backwards when it comes to the march of Islam.

The Six-Day War in June 1967—and Its Aftermath

From a Western point of view, the Arab-Israeli conflict should have disappeared long ago. How could a conflict which has festered so long continue to occupy the world's attention after so many years?

Nineteen years after the 1948 re-establishment of the ancient Jewish state in its ancient homeland, the Arabs again tried to destroy it during the Six-Day war. During the months prior to that war, the Arabs slowly began choking the Jewish state, first with Egypt demanding the withdrawal of the United Nations troops in the Sinai—which separated the Egyptian and Israeli troops—and which also left Israeli shipping through the Red Sea vulnerable to Egyptian attack.

Israel reached out to the international community to honor its commitments to keep open the Straits of Tiran—through which all

Israeli shipping passed on its way to the Red Sea. But the international community reacted in silence.

In a lightening war, Israel not only captured all of the Egyptian Sinai desert, but all of what remained of British-mandated Palestine—*i.e.*, the West Bank and Gaza Strip, and the Golan heights, from which the Syrians at will had lobbed shells down over the Israeli cities, towns and farming communities directly below.

Israel's victory was a tremendous defeat for the Arabs. On June 5, 1967, the war began. In six days, the Israelis inflicted a humiliating defeat on Egypt, Syria, and Jordan. All three Muslim countries lost large and strategically important territory to their non-Muslim (Jewish) enemy.

Israel was elated and strongly believed it now had a chance to sign permanent peace treaties with its Arab neighbors. Its leaders offered to withdraw from almost everything it had conquered in exchange for peace. After all, these Muslim countries had lost the war and clearly could not regain the lost territory militarily. How, from a Western and Israeli point of view, could the Arabs refuse such an agreement?

But that was not to be the case. And it could not be the case, given the Islamic view of the world, which is the best framework for understanding Arab-Israeli conflict. How did this happen?

The 'Three No's'

A few months after the end of the war, the Arab League convened in Khartoum, Sudan, to discuss how they would handle the Israeli victory. All the Arabs—not only the Egyptians, Jordanians and Syrians—at the Arab League Summit in Khartoum, Sudan on September 1, 1967 declared, "Three No's": "no peace with Israel, no recognition of Israel, no negotiations with it."[25]

Israel and the Western world were, to put it mildly, surprised. Why was it more important for the Arabs to cut off their noses and spite their faces by refusing to negotiate with Israel and not regain any of their lost territories? The answer is simple. Had they agreed to sign a permanent peace agreement with Israel in any form, they would have been thoroughly humiliated in almost all of the eyes of their fellow Muslims everywhere. Egypt, Jordan, and Syria were under pressure from their allies to come to some resolution of this conflict. They didn't believe

---

[25] http://www.cfr.org/world/khartoum-resolution/p14841?breadcrumb=%2Fpublication%2Fpublication_list%3Ftype%3Dessential_docu ment%26page%3D69

they could stand up individually against this pressure, which is why they "hid" behind the Arab League's "3 No" resolution. And there was also no way the Arab League—which, with the possible exception of Lebanon, is completely Muslim—could have conceded and recognized Israel's right to exist and to govern a state in the Islamic World.

Why America's Distancing Itself from Israel Makes Muslims More Suspicious of America

Dennis Ross spent years trying to persuade the Arabs and Israelis to get along with each other. But even Ross has been forced to admit that "every Administration that has tried to distance itself from Israel has gained nothing."[26]

Ross is right. Why is this so, and why is it that he and others who clearly have the very best of intentions have failed, whatever America does?

Most importantly, as stated above, Islam divides the world into two peoples: the Muslims and the non-Muslims. From a Muslim perspective, because all Muslims are brothers, they all belong to the same tribe, *i.e.,* they are brothers.[27] All non-Muslims belong to another, distinct nation/people (*millah* in Arabic.)[28]

Muslims learn this from the time they are little, and believe, on some deep level, that all non-Muslims are responsible for each other and look out for each other. The non-Muslims may have internal differences among each other, but, from a Muslim perspective, Muslims see them as one group allied against the Muslims. That is why in the 1980s, so many secular Turkish generals often indicated that we Americans were pro-Greek or pro-Armenian. America, they reasoned was a Christian country, and as such, stood by its fellow Christians against the Turks who were Muslims. When we tried to convince them that this was not necessarily the case, because Americans see Turks, Greeks, and Armenians not as fellow Christians/fellow non-Muslims but as different nationalities, these secular generals heard our words but had great difficulty assimilating what we were saying. This is also why some passionate supporters of the secular Turkish Republic's founder Kemal Atatürk

---

[26] http://www.newsmax.com/Newsfront/Dennis-Ross-White-House-Conscious-Decision-Distant/2016/05/23/id/730197/

[27] There is a common saying among Muslims in Arabic: *"La umam fi'l Islam."* (There are no nations in Islam, i.e., all Muslims belong to one people."

[28] According to the Hadith: *"al-Kufr Millatun Wahida."* (Unbelief is one people/nation.)

would privately criticize him for not having taken Turkey out of Islam and into Christianity. Had he done so, they reasoned, America would see the Turks as fellow Christians and be more sympathetic to Turkish concerns.

At the same time, when non-Muslims don't stand up for each other, those Muslims allied with the U.S. worry about a different problem: If America will not stand up for its fellow non-Muslims against Muslims, then we Muslims certainly cannot rely on America to stand by Muslims whom America claims to support. This stands behind so much of what people in the Gulf countries, the Egyptians, Saudi Arabia, and Pakistan think. Somewhere deep in the recesses of their minds, they instinctively expect us to support Israel, India, Greece, and other countries engaged in battles with Muslims.

There is no way we can win here. It is like a Catch-22. Any support we give to Muslims is suspect. At the same time, they resent the fact that we have supported democracies and non-Muslim countries which share values similar to ours—like democratic India and Israel.

Obama used this logic early on in his Administration when he went to Cairo and gave a speech at Cairo University. He started his speech with the phrase "as-Sallamu 'Aleikum," which is the greeting Muslims use to greet each other. The audience immediately burst out with applause. Why? From a Western perspective, all Obama was doing was saying what so many Westerners believe is how Muslim and Arabic-speaking people greet each other when they meet up. Why the applause for just saying "Hi?"

But this is not true. It is a greeting which Muslims use only among themselves. A Muslim does not use this greeting when meeting a non-Muslim in the Muslim world. Moreover, non-Muslims growing up in the Muslim world know not to use this greeting when talking to Muslims. So from a Muslim perspective, what they understood Obama was saying was that "I" the son of a Muslim which makes me a Muslim in your eyes, greet you as a Muslim. Was that Obama's intention? Who knows? But that is how his Muslim audience understood him.

For a very short while, Muslims seem to have given Obama the benefit of the doubt. There were stories in the Arab world that maybe, even though he said he was a Christian, he really was a Muslim, and just practicing "taqiyya" roughly translated from the Arabic as "dissimilation," which is another weapon/method to advance Islam in the world.

Shortly after the Cairo meeting, Obama traveled to Saudi Arabia and met with the Saudi king to whom he bowed. All of this should have given Obama an edge with the Muslim world. But that is not what happened.

The glow at American recognition at the highest level wore off rather quickly. Thereafter, Obama abandoned these Sunni Muslims and gave in to the demands of the Iranian regime, which though Muslim in our eyes, is Shi'ite, and from the perspective of many Sunnis, Shi'ites are at best apostate Muslims, if not actually non-Muslims.

So, in spite of providing diplomatic, funding, training and weapons support to Sunni al-Qa'ida/Muslim Brotherhood forces in Egypt, Libya and Syria, many perceived that Obama in fact abandoned them by allying the U.S. with the Sunnis' arch enemy the Shi'ite. This, to large numbers of Sunni Muslims, was treachery—and Sunnis comprise about 86% of the entire Muslim world. So Obama tried to fool us, they reasoned. He told us he's one of us and then joined up with the Shi'ite. So many Sunnis see the Shi'ite as non-Muslims. Obama's treachery—again from their perspective—demonstrates to them that he's actually siding with the non-Muslims against them. This is perfidy.

Obama proved to them that he really is a non-Muslim, and that he is allying himself with the non-Muslims against Islam, the natural course of events.

Applying all of the above to the Arab-Israeli issue, Muslims expect that America naturally should ally herself with the non-Muslims, because America is non-Muslim. In this case, America under Obama at first abandoned its natural ally, non-Muslim Israel, and then pretended to ally itself with the true Muslims—*i.e.,* the Sunnis—and then abandoned these Muslims and showed its true colors by allying with the Shi'ite.

This, from a Sunni perspective, should be the natural order of things: the Muslim people vs. the non-Muslim people.

This brings us back to the above-mentioned remarks by Dennis Ross. Throughout the course of Obama's tenure, the administration did its utmost to distance itself from Israel—which, from a Muslim perspective, is part of the same people (*i.e.,* the non-Muslim people). Has it gained us friends and allies in the Muslim world? Many surveys indicate that America is now more hated than it ever was before Obama's time when previous administrations went out of their way to demonstrate their close relationship with Israel. From a Western perspective, this sounds illogical. If we are distancing ourselves from their enemy Israel, shouldn't this make us potentially better friends with Israel's enemies?

What this really demonstrates to the Muslim world is that America—headed by a perfidious (from their perspective) President Obama—was an unreliable ally and a harmless enemy. We Muslims must take cover. America has proven that it won't stand by its natural non-Muslim ally Israel, and will abandon us Sunni Muslims to our fate. No wonder Dennis Ross was right. Abandoning Israel wins America no friends in the Muslim world, and is treated with suspicion for having done so.

America, from a Muslim perspective, must naturally stand with its non-Muslim allies against the Muslims. When it does not, it shows the Muslims how unreliable America is. The proper conclusion we must draw from this is that we should stand by Israel, India, and other non-Muslims because all of us belong to the same people—the non-Muslim people—and are therefore responsible for one another. Muslims and non-Muslims can never really be allies.

Is Zionism Racism?

The UN has been a superb weapon in the conduct of Islamic warfare. The UN passes resolution after resolution against Israel, irrespective of the issue under discussion. If the UN can oppose Israel, it does.

Probably the most famous anti-Israel UN resolution was passed on November 10, 1975. It labels Zionism as racism.[29] Let's examine the facts here in order to determine whether this can be true.

It is simply factually incorrect to say that Zionism is racism. Zionism is the belief that Jews have the right to return to their ancient homeland and the re-constituted entity that their ancestors lost 2,000 years ago, when they were defeated by the Romans. The Jews who choose to exercise that right of return subscribe to that principle. The founders of the Jewish State believed passionately in that mission. Determining who and what is a Jew becomes essential in determining whether Zionism is or is not racism. By the strictest definition of Judaism, a Jew is someone born to a Jewish mother. Traditional Judaism does not concern itself with the religion, ethnicity, or race of the father. That means that the father could be of any background—*i.e.,* European, Asian, Caucasian, black, Indian, American Indian, or whatever.

From this we conclude that the paternal identity of the father is irrelevant in Judaism. Living in the ancient homeland is one of the most

---

[29] https://en.wikipedia.org/wiki/United_Nations_General_Assembly_Resolution_3379

important commandments in Judaism. Zionism is part of Judaism. As such, any child of the above-mentioned mixed background, whatever his father's origin, is, by the Jewish definition, a Jew.

So Zionism cannot be racism because all Jews of Jewish mothers are Jews, irrespective of the father's origins.

As it is obvious that racism has nothing to do with Zionism, why was the resolution passed, and why did Muslim countries push this false resolution so passionately? This UN legislation had nothing to do with truth. At that time, being called a racist was one of the worse epitaphs one could hurl, bordering on an accusation of criminality—which is exactly the reason that the Muslims who supported this resolution chose to push it.

Anything that helped the cause to either put Israel and its supporters on the defensive, or hurt Israel, was and remains fair game. Given the automatic majority that the Muslim world can muster against Israel, it stands to reason that whatever is the latest derogatory label of the day, Israel will be labeled as such. If by some stretch of the imagination, scientists learn that oranges contain a carcinogen, it would not be surprising to see the UN General Assembly pass a resolution condemning Israel for exporting oranges to the world.

For the Muslim world, objective truth doesn't matter. What matters is to use every tool that comes to hand to make the world Muslim. In this context, the UN, the largest international body in existence, is a great platform and venue to help Islam take over the world.

Domination: Islam's Goal is to Dominate America

The Founding Fathers of the U.S. did their best to enshrine the principle of individual liberty. They called for Freedom of Religion and included in the Constitution a clause whereby neither the government, nor by extension any other force, could impose its will on the people when not in time of war.

This has been the basis for the deep American commitment to the principle of live and let live. One could argue that is similar to the Qur'anic principle—To You Your Religion and To Me Mine.[30] But is this

---

[30] Qur'an 109:1-6

really how Islam deals with the non-Muslims and the world which is now dominated by non-Muslim powers?[31]

When the Muslim prophet Muhammad started preaching and seeking converts to his new faith, he was weak and feared that the rulers of Mecca would eliminate him and his followers. In this situation, Muslims believe he received a revelation from Allah which amounts to "live and let live," which the above-mentioned Qur'anic verse seems to call for.

But after Muhammad fled to Medina, he succeeded in creating a state in which he and his followers dominated. In Medina, Muslims believe he received verses which call for Muslim domination of the world.

These two views of the world conflict which each other. It's either live and let live, or I dominate you. How did the Muslims come to terms with these two radically different views of their role in the world? The Muslim authorities who interpreted the Qur'an and Muhammad's intent were forced to rely on traditions about their prophet (called the *Hadiths*), and legal exegeses which interpreted the Qur'an (called *tafsir*).

The way that the later Muslim religious authorities resolved this contradiction, and others like it, was to come up with the following legal principle: When verses appear to contradict each other, those verses revealed during the later period—*i.e.,* in Medina—superseded those which were revealed during the earlier period, *i.e.,* in Mecca. Thus Islam appeared to go from being a "live and let live" faith, to an "I will conquer you and you will live under my rules" faith.

This sharia principle justified Islam's need to dominate others, and dominate the world. It also justified the Muslim need to conquer new lands, and bring them under Muslim rule.

It is in this context that we must understand some of the latest speeches of Islamic jihadis who live in America and who call for Muslim domination of our country. This video clip[32] and transcript[33] demonstrate how this works:

In this video clip and transcript, the American Hizb ut--Tahrir leader exhorts Muslims to refrain from voting in U.S. elections, telling his audience "Islam is here to dominate." American elections, he argues, are one of the ways America makes Muslim assimilate into American

---

[31] Many early commentators actually define this verse as less about 'live and let live' and more about drawing lines of enmity between Muslims and non-Muslims. It's a statement that foreshadows the eventual expression of Al-wala' wa-l-bara']

[32] https://www.youtube.com/watch?v=Eo9ErQdZH-o

[33] http://www.memritv.org/clip_transcript/en/5493.htm

culture. Elections are based on majority rule, which does not apply to Islam until Muslims become the majority. To be sure, many Muslim and non-Muslim Americans are uncomfortable with this reality and consequently go to great lengths to rationalize statements like these. We often hear Muslim apologists say that "X does not speak for Islam, or that all Muslims do not accept what X said." But who are they to decide what the Islamic view is on any issue? Unlike Catholicism which has a Pope who is the final authority for that religion, (Sunni) Islam has no religious hierarchy which determines what is or is not Islamic.

As such we must therefore ask ourselves what is the true meaning of these verses, and how have they been understood historically. Doing so enables us to understand for ourselves what the reality is.

Sadly, for better or for worse, what this Muslim leader calls for in his speech is completely within Islamic tradition. Domination of non-Muslims and coercion of Muslims who disagree with this leader's approach is obligatory within Islam. As Prof. Lewis often said in many of his speeches, this boils down to "I'm right. You're wrong. Go to hell!" Meaning, I will dominate you, and you will do what I demand—or else!

So whatever we think about the harsh direct words about the above-mentioned speaker, he is speaking completely within Islamic tradition. Islam's goal is to dominate America, and eventually the entire world.

Boycott, Divest, and Sanction (BDS)

To varying degrees, many Arabs and Muslims see the BDS movement as another weapon in their Islamic arsenal to eliminate Israel and return that land to the Dar al-Islam. Israel, in any form, is Islamic territory, and therefore belongs to Muslims forever (according to Islam).

Many Arab and Muslim leaders subtly advocate the same goals as many BDS activists: to eliminate Israel as a non-Muslim entity from lands that "belong" to Islam.

Following the al-Aqsa war of terrorism in 2001,[34] senior Muslim Brotherhood jurist Sheikh Yusuf al-Qaradawi published an Islamic legal ruling (*fatwa*) on boycotting Israeli goods.[35] Iranian Supreme Leader Ayatollah Ali Khamenei did the same.[36]

---

[34] https://en.wikipedia.org/wiki/Second_Intifada

[35] http://www.inminds.com/boycott-fatwas.html

[36] http://en.mehrnews.com/news/31711/Leader-issues-fatwa-calling-for-boycott-of-Israeli-goods

Why did these Islamic leaders so strongly support the BDS campaign? For them, the reason is simple: Because the existence of Israel is an affront to Islam, as former Syrian leader Hafez al-Assad, himself an Alawite and therefore not a true Muslim in Sunni eyes, declared throughout his life, any strategy and every tactic to rid the world of Israel is acceptable in service of advancing Islam as a victorious and conquering civilization.[37]

Palestinian affairs analyst Khaled Abu Toameh reminds us of Hamas's support for BDS. He wrote in a Gatestone Institute brief that, "Senior Hamas official Izzat al-Risheq, heaping praise on BDS advocates and activists openly, admitted that the ultimate goal of the BDS campaign was to destroy Israel." Risheq said, "We call for escalating the campaign to isolate the occupation and end the existence of its usurper entity."[38] Yair Lapid, former Israeli finance minister and head of the centrist Yesh Atid Party put it bluntly. In a June 2015 speech he said, "the BDS movement is actually a puppet in a theater operated by Hamas and Islamic Jihad."

Palestinian BDS leader Omar Barghouti has expressed the same view. He has stated in classic Islamic tradition: "Definitely, most definitely we oppose a Jewish state in any part of Palestine. No Palestinian, rational Palestinian, not a sell-out Palestinian, will ever accept a Jewish state in Palestine."[39]

---

[37] http://www.jpost.com/printarticle.aspx?id=439491

[38] http://www.gatestoneinstitute.org/5940/bds-hamas

[39] http://www.voltairenet.org/article153536.html

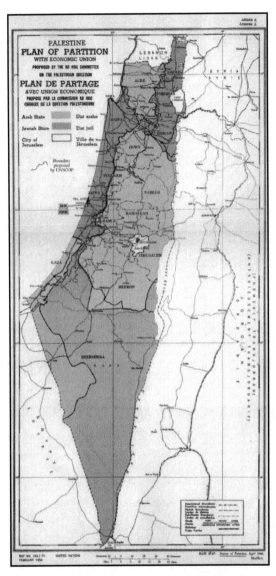

Hamas, Fatah, PLO factions, Islamic State (IS), al-Qa'ida and other jihadi groups believe they are following the rules of warfare laid down by their prophet Muhammad and his companions. These rules are found in the Qur'an, the *hadith*, the sharia and the Sira, the biography of Muhammad written about 150 years after his death.

The Arab (Palestinian)-Israeli conflict is not a political conflict; it is, from these Muslim leaders' point of view, a conflict between Islam—however Islam is defined—and the non-Muslim world. Israel, like Spain, has taken land which belongs to the Muslims—again, from a Muslim point of view. Muslims may not rest until this land is returned to Muslim rule. And by that definition, Israel, irrespective of the size of its borders, meaning even the rump state envisioned by the 1947 UN resolution which called for the creation of a Jewish State and an Arab state in what was mandatory Palestine, is impermissible.[40]

The international BDS campaign is also designed to strike fear in the hearts of Israelis, demoralize them, with the goal of causing the isolation of Israel internally and internationally in order to spur its implosion.

---

[40] https://upload.wikimedia.org/wikipedia/commons/b/bd/UN_Palestine_Partition_Versions_1947.jpg

Leading BDS activists such as As'ad Abu Khalil have confirmed that, "The real aim of BDS is to bring down the State of Israel."[41]

As Abu Toameh has urged us to understand, in Hamas's case, Risheq's remarks reflect Hamas' aspirations that "BDS paves the way for the destruction of Israel through boycotts, divestment and sanctions." Abu Toameh added that "Hamas believes that such tools are no less important than rockets and suicide bombings, which have thus far failed to achieve the goal of wiping Israel off the face of the earth."

Aside from shared goals, how is BDS a weapon in the Islamic arsenal? According to the sharia, anything that spreads Islam can be used. That includes military means, to which the widespread stabbings and beheadings across the Middle East attest. But Islamic warfare also includes "soft power" weapons such as diplomacy, politics and PR campaigns such as BDS and other political initiatives.

The Boycott, Divest, and Sanction Campaign (BDS) is nothing more than the latest weapon that the Muslim world is using against Israel. When this weapon fails, it will be abandoned, at least temporarily, and other weapons will take its place. But if, in the future, the Muslims determine that it can again be useful, we can expect Muslims to again pull it out of its arsenal, and again deploy it as a weapon to de-legitimatize, and hopefully destroy the Jewish state. Anything is fair in this campaign to return what is today Israeli-controlled territory back into the bosom of Islam.

---

[41] https://en.wikipedia.org/wiki/As%27ad_AbuKhalil

TURNING THE WEST/NON-MUSLIM WORLD INTO A WEAPON OF ITS OWN DESTRUCION

When our intellectuals, political leaders, media spokesmen, and others refuse to label the terrorist actions such as the Fort Hood, San Bernardino and Orlando massacres as Islamic terrorism, the spokesmen are turning us against ourselves. We then become a weapon of modern Islamic warfare to destroy ourselves.

The only way we can defeat an enemy is to label him as he sees himself. Refusing to do so means we refuse to take the necessary means against the onslaught from jihadis who seek to destroy our faith in ourselves, and eventually to submit to their will. By constantly rationalizing these terrorists' acts as anything but what they are, we are making our people realize that they cannot rely on our own national leaders to protect us against an enemy which is trying to take us over from within.

Many of these terrorists are American or European born, and for whatever reason, chose to identify with forces which want nothing more than to turn the U.S. and Europe into Islamic territory—*i.e.,* conquering both and turning them into sharia-ruled territory and thus part of the Dar al-Islam.

We must admire their cunning and their ability to turn us against ourselves.

Even more interesting is how many in the Muslim world understand former President Obama. From a Muslim point of view, because his father was a Muslim, he, whatever he says, is also a Muslim. Obama might call himself a Christian, and from a Western point of view, anyone has the right to identify religiously whatever way he chooses.

Consequently, it has been fascinating to follow the debates among Muslims in the Muslim world about who exactly Obama is. During Mr. Obama's first presidential campaign, he told the world that he was a Christian. This was at best puzzling to the Muslims, because they knew he was at least born Muslim because his father was Muslim. Why then did he claim to be a Christian?

On one hand, according to the sharia, the punishment for converting out of Islam (especially after the age of puberty) is death, even without a trial. Often, in history, when someone was suspected of leaving Islam, he was found dead, if he were to be found. To this day, a Muslim woman who married a non-Muslim man can be murdered by her family for doing so—and this is legal under sharia. But if a Muslim man married a non-Muslim woman, then his children are naturally understood to be Muslims.

So where does this leave us with former President Obama? The debate among Muslims in the Muslim world was among those who believed he was pretending to be a Christian, in order to advance Islam. As proof, they cite his above-mentioned Cairo speech which he opened by saying "As-salamu 'Aleikum," which tells his Muslim listeners—again, from their view point—that he is signaling that he is a fellow Muslim. So, was he hiding his 'Muslimness' from his Western audience in order to advance the Islamic cause? If so, that too would be a weapon in the Islamic warfare arsenal, because lulling the West into a false sense of complacency could help the cause. That is called taqiyyah—*i.e.*, dissimulation, which is allowed, even encouraged, by the Qur'an[42] and Sunnah.

If not, *i.e.*, if he really had converted to Christianity, then, the argument goes, he could have issued his own death warrant by claiming to be a Christian.

No matter what the case, many in the Sunni Muslim world have at times, especially before his nuclear deal with Iran, thought him to be one of them, *i.e.*, a Muslim advancing the cause of Islam at the expense of the non-Muslim world and, more specifically, the U.S.A.

---

[42] http://www.jcpa.org/text/iranian_behavior.pdf, p. 11

PSYCHOLOGICAL WARFARE

Psychological warfare is another important weapon in the arsenal of Muslim warfare. From a Western point of view, it is inhumane not to tell one's enemy that he has either captured or holds the bodies of enemy combatants. Refusing to reveal this information is also a violation of international law.

But from a Muslim perspective, this psychological torture is fair game. Iran, for example, has refused to reveal whether Ron Arad, an Israeli captured in southern Lebanon almost thirty years ago,[43] is either still alive, or whether the Iranians have his body. Imagine the feelings his family—mother, father, wife, and child—must be going through every day, not knowing the fate of their loved one.

Israel and the U.S. pride themselves on doing everything they can not to abandon their fellow soldiers and leave them in enemy hands, and are willing to go to great lengths in order to find out the fate of those soldiers and civilians missing in action.

Not so in the Muslim world. Muslim militaries usually ignore their soldiers captured by their enemies—be they Muslim or non-Muslim— and see this as one of the dangers of war, and a price they are willing to pay.

Israel, example, which has had to deal with the Muslim approach more than any other non-Muslim country, has gone to any length it can to gain information about Israelis who, on the battlefield, have been lost and whose fate has not been determined. Israel's enemies—most notably Hamas, Yassir 'Arafat's Fatah, Syria's Hafiz al-Assad, and others—have used this to their advantage, and tried to squeeze out of Israel enormous concessions, just to learn the fate of Israelis either lost in action or whose dead bodies are in enemy possession.

Along the same lines, Israel recently asked Russian President Putin to return an Israeli tank which, in 1982, was captured in a battle at Sultan Yaaqub in Lebanon/Syria. A number of Israeli soldiers died in that attack, but three were seen alive in Syria by an American journalist.[44]Israel lost many soldiers in that battle. That tank contained

---

[43] For the latest developments in the Ron Arad case, see
http://en.farsnews.com/newstext.aspx?nn=13950327000334
[44] https://en.wikipedia.org/wiki/Battle_of_Sultan_Yacoub

the remains of Israeli soldiers who died in that battle. The Syrians captured three Israeli soldiers, whose fate has never been determined.

This is completely against the Geneva Convention. But no one seems to care besides the Israeli government and the grieving families. Arabs have rejoiced that they are suffering. Imagine if American, European, or for that matter Israelis would act like Israel's Syrian foes. The world would roundly condemn any of these non-Muslims for committing such heinous acts. Actually, it condemns all of these non-Muslim forces for actions much less brutal—psychologically or otherwise.

Rarely have Muslims condemned such actions on the part of their fellow Muslims. Is this part of Muslim solidarity against the non-Muslims?

Whatever the case, what is clear is that almost any type of psychological warfare is acceptable, in order to defeat the non-Muslim enemy.

The other thing which might change the situation is if the U.S., Europe, or Israel decided to go for the jugular vein of the leaders of these Muslim countries or organizations, and capture its leaders or the sons of its leaders. Experience shows that when Muslim leaders are confronted with such a reaction, they often give in. Three examples demonstrate this clearly:[45]

The Iranian government held U.S. diplomats hostage, holed up inside what had been the American Embassy, for 444 days, from November 4, 1979, until President Ronald Reagan was inaugurated on January 21, 1981. The Iranians decided they would do the same to the Soviets and took over the Soviet Embassy in Tehran. But the Soviets made it clear to the Iranians that they could, if they so desired, continue to occupy the Soviet Embassy in Tehran, but that if the Iranians did not leave the Embassy in 4 hours, the Soviets would "nuke" Tehran. So much for negotiating "Western style." There was no "give and take" here. The Iranians got the message and backed down.

In the case of the American diplomatic hostages, the Iranians deeply feared that Ronald Reagan might do the same to them if they continued to hold American diplomats hostage. It was therefore no coincidence that about 45 minutes before Mr. Reagan took the oath of office, the American hostages were put on a plane in Tehran. At the exact moment that Reagan was sworn in as President, the American diplomats crossed

---

[45] http://www.gatestoneinstitute.org/1563/negotiating-middle-east

out of Iranian airspace into Turkey. The Iranians saw Reagan as a wild cowboy capable of doing anything.

That reputation was to last until the Beirut bombing in 1982, when Reagan proved, in Iranian eyes, unwilling or unable to stand up against them, and so the Iranians continued on their march to whittle away at American resolve and support in the Muslim world, and cause Iran's enemies to begin to look at how to pacify Iran. Iran's enemies acted as any Middle Eastern or Muslim leader would act—pacify and give in, as little as possible, but remain always on the lookout and watching in fear for what the Iranians might do next.

A third example is even more chilling and instructive: During the above-mentioned American hostage crisis, rumors spread in Beirut—which we have never been able to confirm, but rumors in the Middle East are very often understood as facts—that a Lebanese Shi'ite terrorist group had captured a Soviet diplomat. The Soviets responded in kind. They captured the son of the leader of that group, and sent back to that leader one of his son's testicles. The Soviets made it clear that if their diplomat was not released immediately and unharmed, then the Soviets would continue to send back other body parts of the leader's son, until their diplomat was released. The group's leader quickly released their Soviet captive, and the Soviets then released what was left of the leader's son.

Clearly there is a message here for the non-Muslim world. But are we up to the task? Is our civilization prepared to do what is necessary to defend our civilization? Are our leaders willing to recognize the fact that we are at war with these Muslims—again, not all Muslims—but those who refuse to acknowledge non-Muslims' rights to live in peace and security? The survival of (non-Muslim) Western culture is dependent on that, whether we choose to acknowledge this or not.

Sadly, we are reminded of the conversation with a senior journalist at the Israeli Ha-Aretz newspaper in the early 1980s in Washington. We were talking about developments in then-Israeli-occupied southern Lebanon. This journalist knew Arabic and understood the Arab world and its way of thinking very well. He said clearly and succinctly that Arab culture was brutal and lacked compassion—not only against non-Muslims but against fellow Muslims as well. But what was shocking was not his analysis, but the conclusions he drew from his many interactions with Arabs, and especially with Arab Sunni and Shi'ite Muslims. He said, "The only way to defeat them is through barbarity. I am not prepared to do what is necessary to stop them. I prefer to commit suicide rather than to go against my moral code." Interesting—suicide is preferable to confronting the barbarity of Islamic warfare. That journalist—still writing intermittently for his newspaper—prefers suicide. Let's hope that neither his country nor America and the West follow his lead.

Taking Hostages

As far as we are aware, there is nothing in Islamic doctrine which condones taking hostages. But Islamic culture is much broader and has much deeper roots than does the political doctrine called Islam. Islam inherited hostage taking from the pre-Islamic empires, and integrated it into its culture.

Historically, the governments of many Middle Eastern Muslim empires have taken hostages. It was a way for these empires and their leaders to ensure that political enemies either within their empires, or residing in empires ruled by their enemies, would think twice before revolting or attacking them. In an odd way, one could argue that hostage taking sort of guaranteed the peace, because enemies thought twice before attacking. Islamic history is replete with examples of this practice:

Ottoman rulers would often demand that Christian vassal states along the Ottoman borders give their sons as hostages to the Ottomans. This had the advantage both of guaranteeing that the leaders of these vassal states not revolt, because, if they would do so, they would risk having the Ottomans eliminate the sons that the Ottomans held in their possession.[46]

This practice continued on into the last years of the Ottoman Empire. For example, from the early 1500s until midway through World War I, the Ottomans controlled Mecca, one of the most important cities in the Islamic world. The city itself was controlled by the Hashemite clan of the Quraysh tribe, which could trace its ancestry back to Muhammad.

The Ottomans derived great honor as the Guardians of the two Holy Sites—as do the Saudis today—because they controlled both Mecca and nearby Medina. It was therefore essential that the Ottomans ensure they retained absolute control of these cities.

How then to square the circle? How to retain control yet at the same time ensure that the Hashemites do not revolt against the Ottomans? What the Ottomans did was to bring sons of that family that

---

[46] http://ieg-ego.eu/en/threads/models-and-stereotypes/from-the-turkish-menace-to-orientalism/emrah-safa-gurkan-christian-allies-of-the-ottoman-empire

controlled the holy sites from Mecca to Constantinople, the Ottoman capital, and give them a luxurious palace along the Bosporus, and educated them in the ways of the Empire. But all along, it was clear to the Hashemites in Mecca that they had better not revolt against the Ottomans, because their family members in Istanbul would suffer the consequences.

In a subtle way, all three of these instances are variants of Islamic warfare, which are practiced today as well. From a Western perspective, this is the denial of free will. Individuals, not the groups to which they belong, make decisions for themselves. The idea of holding people hostage, just because they are related to potential enemies and trouble-makers, is abhorrent to the Western mind.

But in the Muslim world, taking hostages has been an important tactic to keep enemies in line since pre-Islamic times.

One could argue that that is essentially what the status of dhimmitude is all about. Islam dictates that Muslims must rule. Non-Muslims who claim a revealed scripture from God prior to the advent of Islam can live under Muslim rule, but only as long as they recognize that the Muslims make the rules, and the non-Muslims must submit to the dictates of their Muslim rulers.

If the Muslims suspected that the non-Muslims had violated any element of the extensive regulations stipulated for *dhimmis*, the historical consequences always involved group punishment and ranged from savage pogroms to outright genocide. One could argue that this is what stood behind the Ottoman massacres of the Christian Armenian population in today's eastern Turkey during World War I. Most Armenians were docile; they understood the limits of what they could do, and acted accordingly.

To be sure, there were Armenian revolutionaries who wanted to carve out an Armenian state from the territory of the (Muslim) Ottoman Empire. Evidence demonstrates that these revolutionaries were encouraged by their (fellow Christian) Russians, who were the mortal enemies of the Ottoman Empire.[47]

As World War I progressed, the Ottomans, as typically, held all Armenians collectively responsible for the destruction of Ottoman rule in today's Eastern Turkey. This was, in classic Middle Eastern terms, guilt by association. So in classic Middle Eastern fashion—again inherited by the Muslims from pre-Islamic Middle Eastern culture—the

---

[47] https://www.youtube.com/watch?v=iZLX4LOQFhk

Ottomans decided to move all of the Armenians away from the Russian border. This type of ethnic cleansing from certain regions dates from Biblical times, when conquerors took relatives of the leaders they defeated back to their capitals, and moved vast sections of the defeated population from one place to another, hoping to be able to secure their newly-conquered domains.

Hostage taking is still an important weapon of Islamic warfare today, as can be witnessed from how the Arabs and Iranians deal with Western hostages. One of the reasons that the Iranians took American diplomats hostage, for example, is because the Iranians believed—correctly, as it turned out—that America would be afraid to attack the Islamic Republic because American citizens might suffer the consequences. The hostage crisis therefore enabled the regime of the Islamic Republic of Iran to consolidate its hold on power in the country, while at the same time keeping the United States at bay.

The same is true regarding the Muslim world's view of and relationship with Israel. The Arabs and Iranians know how important every individual is to the Israelis, which is one of the major reasons they try to take Israelis hostage. Hostage taking, because the Muslims are so weak, has become one of the major goals of Israel's Muslim enemies, because the Muslims know that the Israelis will go to the ends of the earth not to have their citizens killed.

Since hostage taking has become such an important weapon in the Islamic warfare against Israel, Israel's enemies have often gone to great lengths to conceal any information regarding the whereabouts of the Israeli hostages they control, or any information—*i.e.,* whether they exist or not and how many they hold—relating to the hostages. Again, we of the West might consider this a heinous act, but it succeeds in keeping the Israelis at bay, which is the goal of Israel's enemies on its borders.

The only way the West could overcome this means of warfare would be to use overwhelming force to eliminate its Islamic enemies. The Muslims—be they Sunnis or Shi'ites, or Arabs, Turks, or Iranians—have only given up the hostages they hold when they fear that their non-Muslim enemies will destroy them. The following examples demonstrate how this principle works:

1. The end of the Iran-Iraq war in 1988. On July 3, 1988, an American naval vessel—the Vincennes—accidentally downed an Iranian civilian airliner flying from Dubai to Bandar Abbas,

across the Persian Gulf to Iran.[48] The Iranians believed that the Americans deliberately downed the plane and, within a week, the Iranians asked for a ceasefire. As Khomeini said, we had no choice other than to swallow a poison pill, because, the Iranians believed, America did this as a warning of what would happen to the Iranian government if it didn't stop its war against Iraq;

2. The above-mentioned Iranian takeover of the Soviet embassy in Tehran and its consequences;

3. Ronald Reagan's taking the oath of office: The Iranians "knew" that cowboy Reagan would destroy Iran if it didn't release the American hostages;

4. The rumor—true or not—that after the Shi'ites captured a Soviet diplomat in Beirut, the Soviets captured the son of the leader of the Shi'ite group which held the Soviet diplomat, and started dismembering him.

These are just a few of many examples that demonstrate how valuable hostage taking is as a weapon of Islamic warfare. But one can argue that a firm response is the best way to guarantee that Muslims abandon, at least for the foreseeable future, the practice of hostage taking.

"Selling a House to a Jew is a Betrayal of Allah"[49]—Muslims Selling Land to non-Muslims—and Thereby Putting Off the Day when All Muslim Lands under Non-Muslim Control Revert to Islamic Rule

Intimidation is one of the most useful weapons of Islamic warfare. Committed Muslim jihadis use it to put both non-Muslims and Muslims on the defensive, and make their enemies worry about the consequences.

Intimidation is a major component of Palestinian Muslim culture in today's West Bank and Gaza Strip. Anyone who in anyway works with the Israelis risks being labeled a traitor and could suffer greatly as a result, both from the Palestinian Authority in particular and Palestinian Islamic society in general.

One of the most dangerous problems Muslims face in these places is selling land or houses to the Israelis. From a Muslim perspective, the

---

[48] http://www.iranchamber.com/history/articles/shootingdown_iranair_flight655.php

[49] http://www.gatestoneinstitute.org/8300/palestinians-homes-jews

very existence of Israel as a Jewish State on what they hold to be Islamic territory cannot be tolerated. Yet the Jews are so powerful that the Muslims cannot wrest control of that land—meaning all of present-day Israel and the West Bank—from these non-Muslims who, by Islamic law, have no right over what they believe should be under Muslim control.

How can Muslims who don't want to accept the existence of Israel in any form come to grips with the fact that they have little or no control over the future of this land?

One of the ways is to threaten to kill fellow Muslims who step out of line and work with the Jews. These Muslims are labeled collaborators and are threatened with death. Muslims who live in the West Bank and Gaza Strip live in constant fear that they will be labeled as collaborators and killed.

These Muslims know that families with whom they have blood feuds—which is sadly the normal pattern of relationships in much of the Arab world—fear that their enemies will find any way to entice Muslim society in general—whether the Palestinian Authority, Hamas in the Gaza Strip, or more powerful families in whose midst they live—to either eliminate or humiliate them.[50]

One of the many ways of doing so is threatening with death any Muslim (or any Christian living under Palestinian rule) who sells land to the Jews.[51] From an Islamic legal point of view, the land is Muslim, so selling it to the enemy is treachery. The Muslims understand this as taking Muslim land and turning it over to permanent non-Muslim control, which is expressively forbidden by the sharia.

That is why we constantly hear about the Palestinian leadership warning fellow Muslim Arabs and Arabic-speaking Christians with death.

That still has not prevented Muslims from selling land to the Jews. Clearly, sales of this nature do occur, and both the buyers and sellers have developed elaborate ruses to protect the sellers. This often includes having the land be sold to or through third parties, where the Muslims living in houses being sold claim that they are being evicted by the Jewish authorities, even though, from a non-sharia legal perspective, these sales are totally legal. Often, the Muslims selling the houses or land receive safe passage and resettlement in other countries, as well.

---

[50] NOTE: Humiliation in the Arab world is a fate worse than death.

[51] For more on how this works, see Khaled abu Toameh,
http://www.gatestoneinstitute.org/8300/palestinians-homes-jews

Under President Obama, the U.S. government protested sales of this nature, because the sales helped thwart the administration's goal of establishing a Palestinian state on territories many American policy makers have decided belong to a future Palestinian State. That is why the buyers go to such lengths to make sure the sales are absolutely legal according to law; both they and the Israeli government simply want to avoid the wrath of American government officials who have wasted so much time and money monitoring Israeli activities in the West Bank and east Jerusalem.

Homosexuality in Islamic Law

Are homosexuality and transgender persons and activities against Islam? Is Islam's stance on these issues part of Islamic warfare?

From an Islamic perspective, Islam must eventually dominate the entire world. Is this a metaphor for how Islamic culture understands these issues? Since Islam must win, there cannot be any permanent compromise with other religions and philosophies. Islam, in the end, must and will dominate!

How does this drive for domination express itself in Islam's wars against others?

While homosexuality, or any illicit sexual activity as defined in the sharia, is subject to the Qur'an's mandated punishments, such issues came to public attention after the massacre at the Orlando, Florida gay nightclub, 'The Pulse'. What is certain is that the terrorist, an America-born Muslim whose parents immigrated to the U.S. from Afghanistan, pledged alliance to IS and was shouting "Allahu Akbar" (Allah is Greater) as he mowed down his victims at the nightclub.

The murderer clearly committed this horrific act in the name of Islam. Was he correct in stating that what was going on at the nightclub violated Islamic Law? And if so, did he, under Islamic law, have the right to take matters into his own hands and kill and maim his victims?

Islamic religious authorities have, during the past 1400 years, expressed various views on homosexuality, many of which oppose each other. But are these views relevant to what happened in Orlando?

But more importantly, are we asking the right questions regarding Islamic Law on homosexuality and transgenderism? Are these questions regarding the doctrine of Islam, or are they part of a much broader question regarding Islamic culture, which has incorporated many other principles which Muhammad and his companions did not address?

What is homosexuality from a Muslim point of view? Does Islamic culture view this issue in the same way as we in the West understand it? And why do we constantly hear from political figures in the Muslim world that homosexuality does not exist in the Muslim world?[52] Are they right? Is this a problem of the definition of homosexuality? Are the Muslim and Western definitions the same?

The answers to these questions explain how differently Westerners and Muslims view homosexuality, and why gayness has become a weapon for the Muslim fanatics in their battle to impose their will on the entire world.

Much has been written about male same-sex relations throughout Muslim history.[53] Some well-known poets in the Arab world such as al-Jahiz belittled their rivals and enemies using imagery which their readers understood to be accusations of being the "passive partners" in a same-sex male relationship. That, in short, is how so many Muslims living in the traditional lands of Islam understand male same-sex relationships. What matters is not that these relationships occur—most Muslim societies expect that this is a feature of life. But what matters is the role one plays in such a relationship. As long as a male plays the dominant role, no one seems to care. This is evident also from the curses that they use against each other. Throughout the Arab and Iranian worlds, it is common to hear males "calling each other out," where one says to the other: "My sexual organ in your anus." Before the developments of politically correct thought in the West, Westerners by and large thought anyone who would utter such a phrase was shamed.

Not so in the Middle East. There, it is power that matters, and when someone says that phrase, the person shamed is the one to whom that insult was directed. The person who says this is understood as powerful, which people respect. And if a male is raped by another male, the rape victim will almost never tell anyone, because, by admitting what has happened to him, he will bring shame[54] on himself, which is a fate

---

52 Quotes from Ahmadinejad, and Özal about the Turkish military. In 1993, at a speech at the Brookings Institution in 1993, Özal was asked about homosexuality in the Turkish military. He responded: "We have real men in the Turkish military."

53 There is relatively little written about female physical relationships, and these do not seem to pose a problem in Islamic culture.

54 Shame ('Aib (Arabic), Ayip (Turkish), and 'Eyb (in Persian) in the Middle East is understood as what others say about you, not necessarily what you actually do.

worse than death in the Islamic world. Consequently, what one actually does is secondary to what people say he does in that part of the world.

It is against Saudi law, for example, to engage in homosexual acts.[55] In practice, however, society looks the other way. What the Saudi authorities really crack down on is males dressing effeminately, or soliciting males wishing to play the "active role" with another man. As this article describes, gay means a male playing the submissive partner. Any other activity, involving, for example mutual sexual acts without penetration, is not understood as a gay relationship.

So maybe, in Islamic cultural terms, leaders like former Iranian President Ahmadinejad and Turkish Prime Minister Özal were correct. There is relatively little male homosexuality—as they understand it, because it is difficult in those societies to find males willing to play the passive partner.

It is in this context that we should understand the Orlando massacre. We have conflicting versions of what was going on in the mind of Omar Mateen, the killer. To be sure, we know he understood what he was doing in Islamic terms, because of the vocabulary he used both during the killing spree and when he called the police beforehand to inform them what he was about to do. He most definitely understood himself as a jihadi in the service of Allah.

But was something else going on in his mind as well? Evidence demonstrates that he had frequented that nightclub himself. We also know that he had been married, and that he called his wife while he was massacring the people at the club. Was he in Western terms gay? Was he bisexual? Or even more importantly, in the gay relationship he had, was he the "passive partner?"

Could it have been that he engaged in "Islamically shameful" acts and believed that killing others doing the same would expunge his "sins" by killing people engaged in similar acts? From an Islamic cultural as well as legal point of view, he redeemed his honor by killing people engaged in acts which Islam prohibits.

This might sound strange to the Western ear—or maybe even contradictory. But not in an Islamic cultural context. Many of the suicide bombers have been found to have shamed themselves in the eyes of their friends and family. The only way to remove the blotch on their

---

[55] There is a detailed and fascinating study on Homosexuality in Saudi Arabia. See: "The Kingdom in the Closet," http://www.theatlantic.com/magazine/archive/2007/05/the-kingdom-in-the-closet/305774/

honor, or possibly even on their family's honor, was to be a suicide bomber ('martyr') and thereby redeem himself.

Is that how 'Omar Mateen understood himself, his life, and his need to massacre innocent people in the name of Islam?

Whatever the case, and however what went on at the Pulse nightclub is viewed under Islamic Law, clearly Mateen, and others like him see and have seen what he did as a weapon of Islamic warfare against the forces of evil, which, from their perspective, is what Western non-Muslim culture is all about.

As such, it behooves us in the West not to worry about what Islamic Law actually says about homosexuality or transgender relationships. It is not a matter of religion here, but rather of doctrine and law. It is also a matter of Islamic culture, which will use any tool to further its goal to bring the entire world under Islamic rule, and make everyone convert or submit to Islam.

Islam must dominate. It must set the agenda. It must dictate the terms of any relationship. So yes, since anything can be a weapon to advance the spread of Islam, sexuality, as we understand it in the West, is certainly a weapon which can be mustered to bring the world under Islamic domination.

CONCLUSION

G iven all of the above, how can we deal with Islamic warfare? Clearly, we cannot compromise with those who in the long run seek to make all of the non-Muslim world convert to Islam. The Quranic verse stated above,[56] which roughly translates as "Live and let live," seems far from how Muslims have understood Islam since Muhammad created his Islamic state in Medina in the late 620s. Muslims are required to make us succumb to Islam by any means possible. We, however, should not be willing to compromise ourselves out of existence.

From our perspective, people have the right to decide how they should live their lives. Islam, however, requires its adherents to turn the entire planet into one Islamic state—something we cannot except. So are we doomed to fight Islam until the end of time?

How should we address this problem? Both Judaism and the various forms of Christianity have long ago had to re-interpret their traditions in order to survive under conditions beyond their control. Had they not done so, they might not have survived today. Islam, on the other hand, has never had a "reformation" like Judaism and Christianity, its two elder brothers.

Could Islam reform? From personal experience, there are many Muslims who reject violence against non-Muslims and against other Muslims who do not think as they do. Why have they been so hesitant to speak out publicly on this issue? So many of them fear that if they open their mouths and criticize Islam in any way, some of their more militant fellow Muslims might accuse them of apostasy, the punishment for which is death. It is therefore understandable why these Muslims remain silent.[57]

---

[56] Literally, "You have your religion and I have my religion." Qur'an 109:5

[57] For example, I once shared a panel with a long time Muslim friend whom I knew agreed with me on opposing the Muslim fanatics in suburban Paris forcing young women to marry against their will. I spoke first and expected him to support my position by talking about his personal experiences in these Muslim enclaves. Instead, he lambasted me publicly for trying to oppose my non-Muslim Western views on these Muslim women. I was shocked. When he sat down after speaking, I asked him why he said what he said, when we both knew he strongly agreed with me. He looked me straight in the eye and said: "You are not a Muslim and it is expected that you would have these views. By I am a Muslim and if I agreed with you publicly, they might accuse me of being an apostate and assassinate me. So of course, I won't agree with you in public. I want to remain alive!"

Maybe then, the only way Muslims would be willing to re-interpret their sources is when they are forced to do so.

Sadly, the vast majority of Muslims have no incentive to re-examine their sources and find verses in their original sources to enable them to get along with others. By and large, the non-Muslim world has responded to Muslim demands and actions by submitting to these demands. Many non-Muslim countries—no longer committed to their cultures and the values of their founding fathers—are gradually submitting to Islam. Why should most Muslims be willing to reexamine their sources to get along with others when we, their eternal enemy, appear weak and unwilling to stand up for our values and culture? They believe that they are winning.

But are these Muslims right? Are we really unwilling to fight them? Time will tell. But the history of the West tells us something about ourselves. Western actions during the years that led up to World War II might provide us with an answer. When Hitler rose to power, the West essentially did nothing. As Hitler gradually annulled the Versailles Treaty, we looked the other way. In Asia, Japan gradually imposed its will on its neighbors and we did nothing.

But eventually, both the Japanese and the Germans went too far. The UK's Winston Churchill stood alone against the Nazis. But after Japan attacked Pearl Harbor and Hitler declared war on the U.S., we were forced to react. And then, the U.S. turned around and brought the Germans and Japanese to their knees. Only when both countries surrendered in utter humiliation, destruction, and defeat did America help them rebuild.

Are we facing a similar situation today? The more we rationalize what these fanatic Muslims are doing, the more we strengthen them. By refusing to obliterate our fanatic Muslim enemies, the more we seem to be following the World War II example.

But do we have the inner fortitude to stand up and do what is necessary to eradicate our Muslim enemies? Do our societies have the inner will to defend and protect ourselves from the onslaught of supremacist Islam?

The answer remains to be seen. Europe and America do not yet get high marks for their reaction to the march of Islam. The more we look the other way, the more they acquire technologies and abilities with which to inflict enormous damage on us. Our inaction emboldens them.

Our words and verbal threats mean little to them. Arabs, Turks, and Persians all have phrases in their languages which summarize our actions up to now: "empty words." It is action that counts and, much as we might claim to the contrary, we have failed in their eyes to act.

Does this mean that we are headed toward a conflagration? And is conflagration the only way to solve this problem? The way things look today, the sad answer is yes. Had we eliminated Hitler before he acquired the ability to destroy so much of Europe, Europe and the West might look very different today. But we waited too long to do so with the resulting massive loss of life and property everywhere.

But we did eventually react and save the West. Today, our self-appointed elites—our political, intellectual, academic, and economic leaders—by and large have demonstrated that they do not have the will to defend ourselves against the onslaught of the supremacist Islam that wants to overtake us. Our churches are by and large empty, while mosques are springing up all throughout Europe and the Western Hemisphere. Islam is on the march, and Christianity and Judaism outside of Israel are in retreat. The appropriate analogy seems to be "Rome burned while Nero fiddled."

In short, the way events are unfolding, we ARE headed for a catastrophe. Whether we like it or not, we are facing an existential battle with an Islam that intends to dominate us and dictate how we will live. If we don't stand up for ourselves, either we or these Muslims will eventually dominate the other. If we win, it is likely that they will suffer a global defeat. Our natural allies in this battle will be Russia, China, Israel, and whatever other countries and peoples are the enemies of these Muslims. If we defeat these fanatics, those Muslims who do want to get along with everyone else would have the opportunity to safely re-interpret their sources so that the rest of the Muslim world can exist. Otherwise they will continue to be overwhelmingly afraid to do so.

If we do not have the will do to what is necessary to defend ourselves and our civilization, we can expect that with time, probably in the not-too-far-distant future, our descendants will all be Muslims.

ABOUT THE AUTHOR

Harold Rhode received a Ph.D. in Islamic History from Columbia University, and he remains a faithful student of Professor Bernard Lewis. He spent many years living in the Muslim World—learning their respective languages and absorbing their cultures. Rhode served for 28 years in the United States Office of the Secretary of Defense as an advisor on Islamic affairs. He is currently a Distinguished Senior Fellow at the Gatestone Institute.